D1716455

Native North Americans

Arts, Society, and Religion

BROWN
BEAR
BOOKS

Published by Brown Bear Books Limited

An imprint of:
The Brown Reference Group Ltd
68 Topstone Road
Redding
Connecticut 06896
USA
www.brownreference.com

© 2009 The Brown Reference Group Ltd

ISBN: 978-1-933834-79-5

Editorial Director: Lindsey Lowe
Senior Managing Editor: Tim Cooke
Managing Editor: Laura Durman
Editor: Clare Collinson
Designer: Rob Norridge
Picture Researcher: Clare Collinson

Library of Congress Cataloging-in-Publication Data available upon request

Picture Credits

Cover Image
Istockphoto

Alysta/Shutterstock: p.97; Sascha Burkard/Shutterstock: p.68; Steve Byland/Shutterstock: p.73; William J. Carpenter/Library of Congress: p.50; Case & Draper/Library of Congress: p.75; W.C. Chewett/Library of Congress: p.44; Edward S. Curtis/Library of Congress: p.10, p.23, p.24, p.52, p.65, p.81, p.82, p.90, p.91, p.101, p.104; Detroit Photographic Co/Library of Congress: p.33; Henry François Farny/Library of Congress: p.37; Foerster Steffen Photography: p.7; Zack Frank/Shutterstock: p.54; Jose Gil/Shutterstock: p.41; Heyn Photo/Library of Congress: p.19; John K. Hillers/Library of Congress: p.86; Gertrude Käsebier/Library of Congress: p.61; Kavram/Shutterstock: p.99; Library of Congress: p.29, p.88; McKenney & Hall/Library of Congress: p.17, p.20; Photos.com/Jupiterimages Corporation: p.9, p.13, p.79; Louis René Lucien Rollet/Library of Congress: p.31; Dmitry Rukhlenko/Shutterstock: p.77; Simeon Schwemberger/Library of Congress: p.85; Alexey Stiop/Shutterstock: p.47; Isaiah West/Library of Congress: p.71; Winter and Pond/Library of Congress: p.93.

Artwork © The Brown Reference Group Ltd

Printed in the United States of America

Contents

Introduction

The six volumes of *Native North Americans* cover all aspects of the history and culture of native peoples in what are now the United States and Canada. Each volume covers a particular aspect of Native American life: Peoples of the East, Southeast, and Plains; Peoples of the Southwest, West, and North; Arts, Society, and Religion; History; Personalities and Places; and Warfare, Economy, and Technology.

About this set

Each volume in *Native North Americans* features a series of articles arranged in A–Z order. The articles are all listed in the contents pages of each book, and can also be located through the indexes.

Each illustrated article provides a concise but accurate summary of its subject, accompanied where relevant by informative maps. Articles about major tribes are each accompanied by a fact file that provides a summary of essential information.

Within each article, two key aids to learning are located in sidebars in the margins of each page:

Curriculum Context sidebars indicate that a subject has particular relevance to certain key state and national American history guidelines and curricula. They highlight essential information or suggest useful ways for students to consider a subject or to include it in their studies.

Glossary sidebars define key words within the text.

At the end of the book, a summary Glossary lists the key terms defined in the volume. There is also a list of further print and Web-based resources and a full volume index.

About this volume

When the first Europeans arrived in North America and met native peoples, they quickly dismissed them as savages. In fact, native groups had evolved highly sophisticated belief systems and a wide varierty of social organization, and were highly accomplished at forms of cultural expression such as the visual arts, music, and dance.

This book explores these aspects of Native American life among a wide range of peoples. It examines the mythology of different tribes, for example, and how they viewed the cosmos. It highlights the role of spirits in Native American belief and the various ways in which people tried to contact the spirit world. The book also describes the major forms of cultural expression—often closely connected to spiritual beliefs—from quill and beadwork to sand painting. The third broad topic of the volume is the organization of society and the role of individuals within their community and their family or clan. Kinship and status were important in many tribes, as for example expressed in the famous potlatch ceremonies among peoples of the Pacific Northwest.

Afterlife

Many Native Americans believed that life would continue after death. However, ideas of what the afterlife was like varied greatly. Some groups believed that it resembled this world, but with good weather and easy living. Others thought the dead were skeletons who ate "ghost food," such as bark, and spent their time feasting and dancing, with no worries or cares.

Shaman
A person with special powers to access the spirit world and an ability to use magic to heal the sick and control events.

For many Native Americans communication with those in the land of the dead was impossible, but some shamans attempted spirit journeys to recover the souls of the recently deceased and bring people back to life. While on the mystical journey a shaman had to overcome obstacles, such as burning prairies. These supernatural obstacles separated the land of the dead from the living.

Death and reincarnation
The Hopi, who lived in northeastern Arizona, believed in reincarnation—that the soul of a dead person would come back to life in another form or body. However, reincarnation did not happen for everyone.

Those who were most likely to be reincarnated were very young children who had died. The Hopi said that their deaths occurred because they were not ready to live in the present and would be better suited for a future, more peaceful life.

Kachina
A deified spirit believed by the Hopi and other Pueblo peoples to be the ancestor of a human. The term also describes the masked dancers who impersonated the spirits in ceremonies and small wooden dolls that were representations of the spirits.

The spirit world
Others who had been shamans or had held positions of authority might join the spirit world of the *kachinas*. The kachinas were ancestral spirits who controlled many aspects of Hopi life. They were also responsible for bringing rain to make the crops grow. They lived apart from the people for six months of the year, but during festivities were impersonated in the village by dancers wearing masks.

Unlike the Hopi belief in close contact between the living and the dead, most peoples of the Great Plains had only a vague notion of the afterlife. They were, however, careful to avoid burial sites and would often destroy a dead person's property or bury it so that the soul would feel no attachment to the living world. It was believed that a lingering soul was likely to cause trouble. Even mention of the dead person's name was avoided, since the soul, or ghost, might think that someone was calling it back to the tribal village and the living world.

However, some Plains peoples had no fear of the dead. Shamans in the Crow tribe kept skulls to use as oracles in predicting future events. They believed the dead could see and hear everything, even things that would happen in the future. Similar ideas were held by the Haida of the Northwest Coast, who felt that all rights and privileges held in this world came to them from their ancestors. During celebrations, masks representing the ancestors were displayed in the homes of the descendants.

Curriculum Context

A comparative study of beliefs about the afterlife among different groups will help highlight both the connections and contrasts between Native American cultures.

A Native American mask from the Northwest Coast. Many native peoples believed that masks representing their ancestors maintained contact between the dead and the living.

Elaborate ceremonies

Because of this strong belief that the dead could influence the living, most Native Americans held elaborate ceremonies to ensure that the soul departed for the afterlife with happy memories of the people it was leaving behind. The Iroquois, for example, held an annual celebration known as the Feast of the Dead. Although it specifically honored those who had died during the previous 12 months, all the spirits of dead people were invited so that they would know that they were still remembered.

Journey after death

Another means of pleasing the souls of the dead was to ensure they were adequately provided for on their journey from this world to the next. Food, water, moccasins, and items necessary for a long journey were buried with the body. Some groups of the Southeast and Woodland regions made special grave goods from valuable materials. These were used only at burials and were said to please the soul by showing how highly regarded the person had been.

The Maya of southeastern Mexico also believed that a dead spirit made a journey, but that during the journey the spirit was tested by the rulers of the underworld. If it passed the tests, the spirit gained a carefree eternal life. Failure condemned the spirit to wander forever through the underworld, a place from which it could never escape.

For the Aztecs, men who were killed in war gained a special place in the afterlife. They escorted the Sun as it made its way across the sky, then after four years they found eternal life as hummingbirds drinking nectar from flowers. Although this seems a peaceful image, it symbolizes Aztec ideas of warrior power: the flower was a symbol of war, representing the heart of a slain enemy, while the nectar was his blood.

Grave goods

Objects left with the body of a deceased person at the time of burial or cremation. The practice of placing goods with the dead was common in many cultures and beliefs about their purpose varied. Examples included personal possessions of the deceased, textiles, weapons, pottery, and jewelry.

Curriculum Context

Students learning about the civilizations of the Americas may be asked to explore the religious beliefs of the Maya and Aztecs.

Art

Few Native American languages contain words that describe individual objects as works of "art." Words that refer to the making of art as an end in itself are also rare. Yet artists often decorated various everyday objects so that they could be admired for their artistic quality and as a symbol of the tribe's culture.

The means of artistic expression among Native American peoples varied widely, since some raw materials were available only in specific regions. The diverse lifestyles and world views of various Native American groups further influenced artistic output. For example, artists living along the heavily forested seacoast of British Columbia and Alaska often produced huge woodcarvings that represented their ancestors and mythological figures.

Plains-dwelling groups relied on the vast buffalo herds for their survival. As a result, they produced great quantities of embroidered and painted leather and rawhide. The need to follow the buffalo meant that these items had to be lightweight and portable.

Curriculum Context

Students may be asked to identify ways in which artistic output was influenced by the natural environment in Native American societies. The woodcarvings and totem poles of Northwest Coast groups are good examples.

This painting was created by a Sioux artist on buffalo hide. The Sioux and other Plains peoples used buffalo hides and other animal skins to record their history and tell stories.

Pueblo peoples

Village-dwelling peoples of the Southwest, including present-day New Mexico and Arizona.

The Pueblo peoples of the Southwest were farmers who lived in an arid landscape. They made ceramics and textiles that reflected their belief in the spirit world, which controlled the rains necessary for the survival of their crops.

Despite these differences, trade networks did pass on new ideas and raw materials to distant regions, where they affected artistic output. Some new materials were also introduced into Native American art from increased trading with white settlers. Glass beads, manufactured paints and dyes, and iron tools were among the items that greatly influenced the way Native American art forms were created.

Curriculum Context

Artistic expression can be a useful way to study how different native peoples expressed their tribal and individual identities.

Shared identity

Decorative styles shared by a community reflected the common identity of the group. Within these limits artists expressed their own relationship to the natural and spiritual worlds, recorded specific events, and told stories. In this way individual talent was showcased within a general style. In many cultures certain designs were the property of specific artists or their patrons (people who hired artists). Making and decorating clothing also affirmed group identity and membership in certain societies.

A Zuni woman making pottery, photographed in 1903. The Zunis are a Pueblo people from modern-day New Mexico. They are well known for their distinctive pottery, rugs, and baskets, and these art forms still flourish today.

Decline and revival

Before the 20th century Native Americans were often viewed as "crude," "primitive," and "savage" by white colonialists. Few people except curiosity seekers and social scientists collected native-made artworks. At the same time, federal government policies began to promote the erasing of tribal culture and religion and their merging into white society. Making traditional art was discouraged, and artistic production declined.

Early in the 20th century some white artists began to appreciate the value of Native American art. Art education programs for native students were also developed. In the early 1960s the Institute of American Indian Arts was founded in Santa Fe, New Mexico, providing young Native American artists with the opportunity to explore traditional and nontraditional art forms, subjects, and materials. At the same time, mainstream colleges and universities began admitting more Native American students into their studio art programs.

Today the Native American art market is thriving and includes three distinct types of work. These include modern tribal pieces in which the artist uses materials and styles from the European tradition. In these works references to native ancestry may not always be evident. Another type of Native American art uses traditional materials to create items both for family use and for sale. Antique Native American art—traditional items from the historic and prehistoric past—is the third type of work. It commands high and ever-increasing prices in art auction houses in cities such as New York and London.

Curriculum Context

Students might be asked to describe the effects of federal Indian policy including assimilation on Native American tribal identity.

Basketry

Basketry, or the art of making baskets, has always been one of the most beautiful and widespread of Native American crafts. It is also one of the oldest. The first baskets were made in North America in about 7000 BCE. Basketry was almost universally a woman's craft, and skilled basket makers achieved fame for their abilities.

Pre-Contact basketry

In Pre-Contact times there were a number of basket-making communities across North America. In the Southeast the Cherokee, Choctaw, Chickasaw, and Chitimacha were noted basket makers. In the Northwest Coast, the Plateau region, and California basketry was practiced by the Haida, Tlingit, Klikitat, Makah, Wishram, Nez Percé, Yurok, Maidu, and Pomo. The Pueblo, Papago, Pima, and Apache groups of the Southwest were also very creative makers of baskets.

Materials and styles

Tribes in each of the main basketry areas produced distinctive styles. The materials used depended on whatever was available locally. Californian coiled baskets, for example, were made from grass, rush, or shredded yucca leaves, all of which were easy to find. The open-work plaited baskets of the Southeast were made from coarse splints of cane and oak. The Nez Percé made soft, flexible carrying basket-bags from rushes and corn husks.

Baskets for cooking

The finest baskets were woven so tightly that they could hold water and were used for cooking by the "hot-stone" method. In this technique heated stones were added to a liquid to bring it to the boil. This avoided putting the basket on direct heat. Other groups made baskets waterproof by lining them with pitch, a substance usually made from tar.

Curriculum Context

A study of the different materials used in Native American basketry will help students gain an understanding of the factors that affect artistic output in different communities.

A basket made by a member of the Wappo group, natives of modern-day northern California. Wappo basket makers wove baskets so tightly that they could hold water.

Basket designs and decoration

Besides being functional, baskets were nearly always finely decorated, such as with interwoven light and dark materials to make geometric designs.

The coordination of hand and eye needed to produce perfectly uniform weaves and repeating patterns is very demanding. Some of the most remarkable baskets are the tiny ones from California, which were made as a test of the maker's skill. Some of these contain as many as a hundred stitches to the inch (2.5 cm). They are so tiny that it is necessary to use a magnifying lens to count individual stitches.

Modern basketry

The age-old craft of basketry has now largely disappeared among many Native American tribes. Most modern-day Native Americans have replaced hand-woven baskets with metal kettles and pots for everyday domestic use. However, the art of basketry is still being practiced by a few native peoples. Some of the more noteworthy modern basket-making groups include the Jicarilla Apache, some of the Californian tribes, and the Hopi of the Southwest.

Curriculum Context

Students may be asked to explore the techniques used by different cultures to create objects for functional and non-functional purposes.

Birth Customs

In general, most Native Americans saw birth as one of the four most important stages of human life—the others were puberty, adulthood, and death. Some tribes marked a birth with ceremonies or rituals that emphasized its importance to the community. The ceremonies were also intended to ensure that the child would live a long and healthy life.

Curriculum Context

Birth customs are one way in which it is possible to see the close link between the folklore and traditions of Native American communities and the landscapes in which they lived.

Amulet

An object worn as a charm to protect the wearer against evil.

Different habits

Some Native Americans performed ceremonies that they believed could predict an unborn child's future. On the Great Plains, for example, a pregnant woman would leave a toy bow and arrows (symbolizing a boy) and a doll (for a girl) close to a sacred spring. The woman hoped that the spirits would take one of the items before the child was born. This, the Plains people believed, could foretell the baby's gender. If, however, neither of the items was taken, people feared that the spirits did not favor the unborn child, who might be born dead or die young.

Some of the birth ceremonies were very simple. The Iroquois of the eastern Woodland region did not have any direct ceremony at all. However, after the birth of an Iroquoian child the mother was forced to live apart from the daily life of the village, and various charms and amulets were placed around the baby's cradle. The Huron, who lived in the southeast Woodland region, would pierce the infant's ears soon after the birth.

On the Caribbean island of Hispaniola (which is today made up of the Dominican Republic and Haiti) men of the Arawak—one of the first peoples encountered by Christopher Columbus—would sing and dance outside the home in which the mother was giving birth. The men would make as much noise as possible in the belief that the din would drive away the mother's labor pains.

Thousands of miles to the north the Inuit of the Arctic regions of far North America linked birth directly to a naming ceremony. First, the Inuit mother was placed in a small hut or a tent; then, as she suffered from the pains of giving birth, she cried out a series of names. If she cried out a name and her pain became easier to bear, or if the baby began to emerge more rapidly, then that name would be given to the baby. For a period after the birth an Inuit mother was excused from many domestic chores, especially tasks involving the preparation of food.

The Native Americans who lived in the southeast Woodland region believed that water was a powerful spiritual force. The mother, once her birth labor had begun, was placed in a special small house in which women were also required to live during their monthly menstruation. Once the baby was born, but before it was allowed to nurse at the mother's breast, it was taken to a nearby spring or creek. Here it was completely immersed and cleansed in the running water. Immediately after the cleansing, the baby had sacred bear oil rubbed all over its body. Then the ritual duties passed to the child's father, who had to fast for several days as a symbol of sacrifice.

Aztec
Term used to describe the people who were dominant in central Mexico before the Spanish conquest in the 16th century.

Aztec rituals

In Mexico the Aztecs had some highly developed birth rituals. For women, giving birth was seen as the counterpart to the male activity of warfare. The woman who was about to give birth was thought to be no longer in control of her body, which had been possessed by a kind of supernatural or spirit force. Once the infant was born, the midwife who had assisted in the birth shouted war cries that were commonly used by Aztec warriors in battle.

If the newborn baby was a boy, then he was told right away of his responsibilities to society as an Aztec

Curriculum Context

Students may be required to evaluate the importance that different cultures place on rituals. The birth rituals of the Aztecs were a significant element in defining gender roles and the shape of society.

warrior, and the mother was discouraged from expecting any kind of permanent relationship with him. His future lay outside the home, and he was already being taught to look forward to the day when he would leave to fight—and possibly die—in battle. The boy's umbilical cord was often given to a warrior member of the family to be dropped on a battlefield in order to establish a spiritual link with the bloody work of warfare.

For the Aztec father to see the newborn, whether it was a boy or girl, was an emotional moment of a different kind. The father was encouraged to hold the newborn and to run his hands over its body in order to establish an immediate physical bond. Other members of the family would follow suit.

Plenty in a name

Native Americans often had many different names throughout their lives. Children were given a name chosen by a respected grandparent shortly after birth. In some groups the name of a deceased family member who had had a long and successful life was sometimes given to a child. It was believed that the spirit of the family member would safeguard the child's future. The Cree of the Subarctic region took this ancestral naming even further. A newborn baby would be given the name of a deceased family member whom the baby resembled, regardless of gender. At age four or five, when a child's ears were ceremonially pierced, it was given another name. A young person usually had a third name by the time he or she reached puberty. This would have been the final name change for most girls, but boys could have further name changes, depending on their deeds of valor and cunning.

Body Adornment

Native Americans used a great variety of methods of body decoration and adornment, both to enhance their appearance and to emphasize their status or to show to which family or tribe they belonged. In most groups, specialized use of body-paints and facepaints was connected with specific rituals, religious ceremonies and performances, warfare, and even mourning.

Painting—using mineral colors that were mixed with animal fats—was perhaps the most widely employed method of personal decoration. Paints belonged to individuals—although recent research suggests they also may have had tribal significance—and were almost exclusively applied by men.

Women usually restricted painting to their hair parting, which was often colored red, or they wore small, circular marks on their cheeks, placed there by their husbands as tokens of affection. In addition to their everyday painting, most men also owned special paints associated with visions or with ceremonial privileges. Many of these special paints related to warfare, particularly among groups of the Great Plains.

Curriculum Context

Body painting is a good example of a form of artistic expression used by Native Americans to reflect their tribal and individual identities.

A Winnebago chief, depicted in a lithograph from 1844. Among many Native American groups it was custom for warriors to assert their pride and honor by painting themselves with different designs.

Marked for life

A more permanent sign of an individual's identity was provided by tattoos. These were made by puncturing the skin with a sharp instrument, often a form of multi-pointed tattooing needle that was usually owned by a shaman (medicine man). Soot or dyes were rubbed into the skin punctures to produce dark-colored patterns. Both men and women wore tattoos. Often, these tattoos indicated a man's or woman's status within their family and the group.

Curriculum Context

The practice of tattooing large areas of skin by native peoples was common around the globe in warmer areas where people needed less clothing. It is an example of how a group's traditions and forms of self-expression were influenced by the natural environment.

Among some peoples, particularly those of Florida and the Southeast, the subtropical weather meant that people wore very few clothes. The large areas of exposed skin were elaborately adorned, and full facial and body tattooing was common practice. The Florida tribes, such as the Timucua, also practiced other forms of permanent body change: Timucuan men and women had their teeth filed to triangular points and used permanent dyes to turn their lips blue.

Hair care

Less permanent but equally dramatic was the styling and decoration of face and body hair. Native Americans usually have little body hair—most men, for example, find it difficult if not impossible to grow a beard. Body hair was therefore considered "unnatural," and even

Extreme fashion

More extreme ways of identifying status were used by the Inuit and groups of the Northwest Coast. In these areas rings or bones were passed through the septum (inside centerpiece) of the nose, and labrets (lip plugs) made of bone or wood were inserted into cuts through the lower lip. Head flattening was also a custom on the Northwest Coast. This was achieved by fastening a board to the front of an infant's cradleboard while the bones of the skull and forehead were still soft and moldable. This flattened the frontal bones and gave the head a pointed or conelike appearance. Such flattening was believed to improve not only physical beauty but also wisdom and intelligence.

Hair had symbolic importance in many Native American groups. Sioux men wore their hair long and only cut it as a sign of grief or shame. The appearance was often refined by the addition of feathers and other ornaments.

sparse growth was removed by plucking. Shell, bone, or wood tweezers were a common item among the men of many tribes. Some Plains peoples took the removal of hair to the extreme by plucking not only their beards but also their eyebrows.

Nevertheless, most attention was lavished on head hair, which was considered to be a symbol of strength and individuality, as well as the seat of a person's soul. Elaborate and distinctive hairstyles were a common feature in Pre-Contact times. The Crow, a people of the northern Plains, were known for plastering their hair above the forehead with white clay and would comb it back to form a crest. They also added lengths of human or animal hair to the hair on the backs of their heads so that it trailed on the ground behind them. Other groups of the Woodland region, as well as the seminomadic peoples of the Plains, wore their hair in a roach.

Roach

A hairstyle in which the head is shaved except for a strip from front to back across the top of the head.

Black Hawk, chief of the Sauk and Fox, was responsible for a series of battles with U.S. troops before being defeated at the Battle of Bad Axe. In this painting from 1837 Black Hawk's appearance is striking, with shaved head, red, plumagelike hair, and pierced ears.

Gorget

A piece of armor used to protect the throat.

Various types of jewelry

Almost all Native American men and women had pierced ears, from which a multitude of beads, rings, and feathers were suspended. The weight of these ornaments was often so heavy that the lobe of the ear became stretched and formed a long loop. Necklaces, armbands, breastplates, or gorgets, and headbands made from hide, cloth, animal teeth and claws, shells, wood, bone, and copper were regularly worn in Pre-Contact times. These were supplemented by beads, silver, gold, and other items introduced through trading in the Post-Contact period.

Body adornment today

Although modern Native Americans no longer practice the extremes of head flattening, tattooing, and the plucking of all body hair, they still place an emphasis on their appearance. Traditional body- and facepaints have to some extent been replaced by a more generalized Pan-Indian form of painting, but attention to hair and the wearing of numerous ornaments and decorative trinkets is common practice at present-day powwows and native gatherings.

Children

In most cases the wishes and expectations of children were, and are, respected by Native American parents and grandparents. Children usually enjoy a freedom that would rarely be indulged by a family of traditional European or Western upbringing. However, they are also taught respect, honor, and obedience, and to take individual pride in their own achievements.

Shared parenting

In the traditional Native American household both parents were often engaged in many different daily activities. This made it difficult, if not impossible, for parents to give their sole attention to all of the needs of a child and the practicalities of childcare. In former times husbands were frequently away from villages and camps for extended periods, while all the domestic duties—including the preparation of hides and the manufacture of baskets or other goods for trade and sale—were the responsibility of their wives.

By far the majority of Native Americans, however, lived in extended family units with grandparents. Although they may have been too elderly or frail to carry out exhausting daily tasks, grandparents were nevertheless available to look after and teach their grandchildren. Most grandparents, even today, either live in the same household as their own children or are never far away. For many Native American boys the closest family adult relative is a grandfather, whereas girls will turn to a grandmother in times of need.

This does not mean that fathers and mothers are neglectful parents. On the contrary, they are generally indulgent rather than harsh and hesitant in putting any restriction on their children's activities. But it is the grandparents who give the children constant attention.

Curriculum Context

Students learning about gender roles in Native American societies might be asked to focus on approaches to childcare.

Rituals at birth

At birth in some peoples, experienced midwives—usually honored elderly women—assist in the delivery and offer prayers for the well-being and health of the newborn baby and its mother. This might be followed soon after by a request from the father for a respected tribal member, again often an honored woman, to give the baby its first childhood name. When the child is four or five years old, a shaman (medicine man) is asked to give a formal name and to oversee the piercing of the child's ears. This is a public ceremony at which the child is officially "adopted" into the care of the tribe. A show of bravery, such as not crying when the piercing is carried out, may suggest good fortune in the child's life.

Gentle persuasion

By this age a child has already been gently taught in many groups that tears and tantrums will have no effect on parents, grandparents, or other adults who have the child's best interests at heart. Good behavior is usually recognized and rewarded, and although bad behavior is never physically punished—it is abhorrent to a Native American family to strike a child—the child is ignored until such time as his or her behavior improves. If there is no improvement in behavior, any adult approached by the child may hide behind a raised robe or blanket. In this way the child quickly learns that misbehavior results in being excluded from the affection and positive attention of the family circle.

In Pre-Contact times children gained their skills at the feet of their grandparents. A boy's first bow was made by his grandfather, who took him on rabbit and bird hunts close to the village and instructed him in the various tracks animals make and how to approach them unseen. A girl learned her skills from her grandmother, who made dolls for her and provided porcupine quills and the girl's first awl (a tool like a needle) when teaching the child the art of embroidery.

Curriculum Context

A study of how traditions and values are passed on from one generation to the next in different societies will help students understand the importance to many Native Americans of tribal heritage and identity.

This photograph, taken in 1926, shows a mother and baby from the Achomawi of northeastern California. In many Native American societies mothers traditionally carried their babies in cradleboards.

The parents' pride in their children's achievements was often demonstrated through public displays. A boy's first good hunt, even though he may have caught only a couple of small birds, was made into a "feast" to which prominent members of the group were invited. A girl's first attempt at a strip of beadwork or quillwork, no matter how loosely woven, was sewn on the seam of her father's ceremonial shirt. He would proudly wear it through the camp so that everyone might recognize his daughter's work and share in her joy at having made something her father would cherish.

The favored child

At times indulgence of children went far beyond usual parental pride. In some tribes the *Minipoka* might be waited on hand and foot and protected to the extent that he or she learned no useful skills. The Minipoka was dressed only in the softest hides and furs, richly decorated with beads, quills, or with even more valuable elk teeth. The boy favorite did not need to learn how to hunt, since everything was provided, and the girl could depend on her relatives to supply everything she required without effort on her part.

Minipoka

In some Native American groups, a favored child, usually the son or daughter of a wealthy and respected family.

Obligations and respect

The tradition of the Minipoka was actually an exaggerated form of the general high regard in which children were held. To gain their parents' and grandparents' trust and affection, children did, of course, have obligations they needed to accept. Respect for one's elders was primary among these, as was a willingness to anticipate a task that required doing and to set about it without waiting to be asked.

Similar attitudes often prevail in modern Native American families, where an outsider may be surprised by the freedom enjoyed and independence shown by the children. For many peoples individual responsibility and freedom of action combined with respect for the actions and beliefs of others were, and are, of utmost importance in the training and upbringing of their children.

Curriculum Context

The freedom and independence enjoyed by Native American children can be contrasted with the stricter cultural and social values of other contemporary societies.

This boy, photographed in 1910 wearing traditional costume and headdress, is from the Salish group of the Northwest Coast. Salish children were taught from an early age to respect their elders and were given instruction about tribal customs and rituals.

Clan

A clan is a social unit containing several families related through a mother or father. The families share certain privileges, such as the right to control particular ceremonies. Some clans may also claim descent from the same ancestor in the distant past. Clans cross the boundaries of blood and marriage ties, and include members who might come from other areas of the tribal lands.

Social relations among native peoples are often organized along the lines of clan membership. In this way a man may be limited in his choice of wife to a woman from a clan different from his own.

Clans may be further organized into two moieties, or parts. Each moiety consists of several clans that consider themselves closely related to one another. Several tribes may have similar clans and moieties, and individuals will feel a special relationship to these "clan brothers."

A member of a Northwest Coast tribe who belongs to a clan of the killer whales will be welcomed among the killer whale clans of other tribes, although they might speak different languages or be traditional enemies.

Clan names

Clan membership plays a vital role for most Native Americans, whether their original way of life was based on nomadic hunting or on settled farming communities. Often, clans are named after animals thought to have given power to an ancestor.

Among hunting groups these are often the predatory animals and birds. In agricultural groups the clan ancestors may be more abstract forces, such as rain or hail. The members of the clan are thought to inherit special powers to enlist the help of these ancestors.

Moiety

One of two units into which a tribe or community is divided on the basis of descent through one line to a common ancestor.

Curriculum Context

The naming of clans after animals is an example of how Native American attitudes toward nature are reflected in their traditions and practices.

Kivas and clan priests

A good example of the way that clans function is found among the Pueblo peoples of the Southwest. Here a man marries into his wife's clan, which is different from his own, but retains very strong links with his own clan.

Each Pueblo village has a number of kivas. Each kiva is owned by a clan. Thus the kiva brings together men who have married into different families in the village but who also claim membership in the same clan.

The kiva also has its own clan priests who are responsible for specific aspects of the ritual and ceremonial life of the village. In this way a balance is maintained between political authority (through a chief and council elected by the whole village) and ritual authority (as directed by the clans).

Balance of power

The moieties, or divisions of clans into two groups, also help maintain a harmonious balance of power throughout the year.

Each moiety is responsible for the collective efforts of its member clans. This often means that one moiety controls all ritual activity during the summer months, when crops are cultivated and harvested. The other controls the winter season, when the land is prepared for the next season.

Kiva

In Pueblo villages, a chamber built into the ground that acts as a meeting place and ceremonial house.

Cosmology

The word *cosmology* is derived from two ancient Greek words: cosmos, meaning the sky, stars, and planets; and logos, meaning knowledge. The word generally refers to human beliefs about the universe. Native Americans had a number of theories about the universe. Many of these were based on the movements of the stars and planets.

Watching the skies

Astronomical observations made by Native Americans were often more advanced than those made by late 15th-century Europeans. Many Native American ideas about the universe were expressed in mythological terms. The Morning Star (the planet Venus) was often thought of as a warrior who cleared the sky before the sun's return from the underworld at the start of each new day.

In the 16th and 17th centuries, when Europeans began colonizing North America, Old World astronomers dismissed Native American ideas. Yet many tribes could calculate the exact length of the solar year (the time it takes for the Earth to travel once around the sun) with remarkable precision.

Native American universe

The Native American view of the cosmos was reflected in many aspects of daily life. The arrangement of Pawnee lodges, for example, was based on the shape of star constellations in the sky. Native Americans arranged their tepees so the entrance flaps opened to face the rising sun each morning. In this way they symbolically welcomed the life brought by the sun.

To native peoples the world was a sacred place in which everything had a soul. They felt that all life was related, and that each part was dependent on every

Curriculum Context

Students learning about Pre-Columbian America can use diverse beliefs about the universe to explore the differences and similarities between native cultures.

Tepee

A cone-shaped tent built with a pole framework and traditionally covered with animal skins.

other part. According to this view, people were merely another element, no better or worse than anything else. A mouse had its own importance and dignity, as did an eagle or a man, and therefore deserved respect.

The series of worlds

Native American people thought that the present world was merely one of a series of worlds through which people and animals would pass. Many groups believed that there were three worlds. In the upper world dwelt the spirits of those who had lived honorably. A middle world, the present, was occupied by people. The mysterious lower world (or underworld) held many dangers.

As the people moved through these different worlds, they became more human. In the first worlds there was little difference between people and animals. They lived in the same village and spoke the same language. In these early worlds, animals and people might even have married each other.

One reason for the respect shown to animals by Native Americans is the belief that they share common ancestors from the first worlds. Many groups believed a link still existed between these worlds.

Sun Dance lodges

The Lakota Sioux of the Great Plains built ceremonial lodges, known as Sun Dance lodges, around a central pole that represented an axis joining the series of worlds. The center pole was the focus for complex religious ceremonies. It was hung with various symbols and offerings to the animal and plant powers on which the Lakota relied.

Compass bearings

The four cardinal directions (north, south, east, and west) were often associated with other things that

Sun Dance

An important ceremony practiced by Plains peoples to celebrate the renewal of nature.

The building of a Sun Dance lodge was an important part of the Sun Dance ceremony for the Lakota Sioux and other Plains peoples. The central pole served to remind people of the connection between humans and the rest of the universe.

affected people's lives. North, for instance, is the direction from which cold rains and blizzards come and was therefore thought of as the direction of starvation and disease. The four directions also matched the life stages of every living thing, from birth in the east to youth in the south, maturity in the west, and old age and death in the north. These cycles were constantly repeated as the universe was remade again and again.

Mayan calendars

In Mesoamerica the Maya made extensive calculations to create calendars. These were highly accurate and were used to calculate the correct times for planting and harvest. They also gave the Maya a yearly cycle of important ceremonial events that had to be carried out on specific days.

Mesoamerica
The cultural area extending from central Mexico to Nicaragua.

The Maya used two calendars, one of 365 days—the length of the solar year—and one of 260 days. These calendars coincided only once every 52 years. It was thought that on these occasions the Mayan world would either be renewed or be destroyed. The later Aztecs adopted the Mayan calendar. The arrival of Spanish in the 16th century, which led to the overthrow of the Aztec empire, occurred in a year when the two calendars coincided.

Curriculum Context

Studies of the overthrow of the Aztec empire by a small Spanish force should consider the role played by the Aztec belief in a coming world upheaval.

The "Great Spirit"

All Native American peoples believed in a basic spiritual force that was present throughout creation. When native characters on television or in films refer to the "Great Spirit," it is often an attempt to suggest this metaphysical idea. Different peoples called this life force by different names. Woodland Iroquois and Algonquian tribes believed in something called "orenda," or "manitou," which the first Europeans in North America believed was one of their gods. In fact, it represents something very different.

Orenda–manitou does not have a personality in the way the Christian tradition regards God. Some Europeans took orenda–manitou to mean "medicine"—meaning something vague but powerful—which is closer to the Native American sense. There is some of orenda–manitou in every living thing, though some people are thought to have more of the spirit in them than others. This implies that all of nature is sacred. This idea was summed up by Thomas Yellowtail, a Crow shaman (medicine man), in his 1991 autobiography: "[A person's] attitude toward the Nature around them and the animals in Nature is of special importance, because as we respect our created world, so also do we show respect to the real world we cannot see."

Dance

Native Americans have a rich culture of dance, which often forms part of complex religious rituals. Dancing is a way for Native Americans to communicate with the spirit world. It may be done in the open air or within a lodge. Certain dances are performed for specific festivals only. Others are tied to particular events in life or social situations.

Some dances are for individuals; others for societies or whole communities. In each case the act of dancing is believed to unite the human and spirit worlds.

Drumming and chanting

Native American dancing is almost always accompanied by drumming. There might be several drummers, or a solo dancer might also accompany him- or herself on a drum. Rattles are also often used, made from objects such as turtle shells or deer hoofs. There is almost always some kind of singing or chanting accompanying the dance.

Curriculum Context

Students learning about the historical and cultural dimensions of dance may be asked to compare different forms of musical accompaniment and how they relate to particular dances.

A warrior from the Hidatsa tribe, a Plains people from North Dakota, performs the Dog Dance. Native American dancers often wear special clothes and headdresses to represent animals or for symbolic effect.

Dance movements

The dance usually follows a circular pattern, which can be either clockwise or counterclockwise. For Native Americans the dance pattern would be either "with" or "against" the direction of the sun as it moves across the sky. As a rule hunter–gatherers or nomads dance in a clockwise direction, while farming tribes dance in a counterclockwise direction.

The movements made during a dance are of great importance. In the European tradition movements in dance tend to be upward, with the dancers leaping as if to release themselves from the Earth. Native Americans tend to stamp their feet to bring themselves closer to the Earth and the underworld.

Native Americans also tend to lean forward in their dancing. However, whereas male dancers usually make confident, even violent, gestures with their arms and the body (especially in war dances), female dancers are more erect and move their arms less.

Masks

Dancers often wear masks, notably among the groups of the Southwest. The masks may represent animals or spirit forces. To the Native American onlooker a dancer wearing a mask may actually become whatever the mask is said to represent.

Special clothing

As well as wearing masks, the dancers wear special clothes or paint their bodies in a particular way for symbolic effect. During the dance of the summer solstice (the longest day in the year) the Hopi hang spruce branches from their belts, symbolizing long life. Their faces are painted blue on one side (for the sky) and yellow on the other (for corn). A red arc on a white background, which may symbolize a rainbow, is sometimes painted on the forehead.

Hunter–gatherers

People who obtain most of their food by hunting wild animals and eating plants gathered from the wild.

Curriculum Context

Students may be asked to examine how movement and costumes reflect the function of dance in different communities.

These Hopi men, natives of Arizona, are performing an annual snake dance, one of the group's most important and elaborate ceremonies for bringing rain.

Messages to the spirit world

Among settled agricultural peoples, dances are used to ask the spirit world for benefits to the community. The Pueblo peoples of the Southwest have kept many details of their religious practices secret, although more is known of their public dances. In one dance two performers dressed as Pueblo clowns throw ashes into the air to represent clouds, while gesturing as if looking into the far distance. The dancers are believed to be looking for the approach of the rain gods. The call for rain is very important in this dry area of the world.

Native Americans who lived the unsettled life of hunter–gatherers also performed ritual dances to appease spirits. The Inuit of Alaska performed a miming dance before a whaling expedition. While the Pueblo used ash to represent the clouds, the Inuit scattered ashes on the water in order to chase away any evil spirits. If a whale was caught, the Inuit performed a celebration dance.

A similar sort of ritual is still practiced by the Tolowa of California. They perform a special dance when the salmon-fishing season begins. The first salmon is eaten in a special ritual, and afterward the whole group may catch the fish without fear of offending the spirit world. The Coast Salish, a group that lived south of the Kwakiutl in present-day Washington state, performed the Spirit Canoe Dance. The purpose of the dance was to cure people of their illness. Through dance a tribal shaman (medicine man) acted out a journey into the spirit world. The ceremony used carved wooden boards and carved wooden figures. The Salish thought that the objects could bridge the barrier between the spirit and the natural worlds.

The Iroquois of upstate New York had a similar ritual. They believed that an angry bear-spirit would cause mental disorders to break out. Pairs of dancers would perform a dance to calm the bear-spirit.

Sacrifice dances

The great cities of Mesoamerica (the area from central Mexico to Nicaragua) were the scenes of very complicated dance rituals that were performed alongside religious ceremonies. Dancers would perform on the terraces of the pyramids so that the crowds below could see them easily.

These dance rituals could often be gruesome. The priests of the Aztecs, for example, would flay the skin off a sacrificed human and then put it on themselves. This was regarded as a great honor to the victim. In the Mayan civilization dancers mutilated themselves in order to bring blood to the surface of their skin. They would then whirl round and round, so that the blood flowed more freely out of their self-inflicted wounds, creating a dramatic and frightening display.

Death Customs

Death was one of the four important life events—together with birth, puberty, and adulthood—and was often marked by elaborate rituals in Native American societies. For Native Americans the spirit world was present in the natural world, and their death customs were a way of ensuring that the inhabitants of both worlds respected the boundary between the two.

Early rituals

Well before the 17th century groups such as the Creek and the Cherokee of the Carolinas and Georgia had established rituals that marked the social status of the dead person. A dead chief might be mummified, for example, and his body attended by servants in a temple. It was not unusual for relatives or close friends to ask to be put to death so that they could accompany the dead person to the next life.

If the dead body was buried, after a few months it would be dug up again. The bones would then be cleaned and placed in a box inside a temple to the sun god. Other people would be buried in shallow graves or wrapped in skins and left to decompose, as was the practice with Plains tribes.

Giving thanks

One of the most important death customs was that performed by Native American hunters who had killed their prey. This ritual has been shown in several television programs and movies such as *The Last of the Mohicans*. The successful hunters recite a prayer in honor of the dead or dying animal, thanking the spirit world for providing them with food and hides.

Sometimes, after the hunters had skinned and butchered the animal, they reassembled the bones, except for the skull, and buried them. They then stuck

Curriculum Context

A study of diverse attitudes toward important events such as death in different groups is key to understanding their beliefs and values.

the skull on a pole and placed it in the ground to mark the grave site. Native Americans thought that showing such respect to the animal would make sure that there would be more in the future to hunt.

Death rituals in time of war

The scalping that horrified the European explorers and settlers who came to the Americas during the 16th and 17th centuries was a ritual action. The intent was to prove that an enemy had been defeated and killed in battle. Sometimes these scalps were taken from someone who lived to tell the tale—someone who may merely have been badly wounded or stunned.

More gruesome tortures were performed on prisoners by groups such as the Apache. These were often carried out in response to atrocities committed against them by enemies. Apache war parties went on raiding expeditions mainly for economic reasons. They did not take scalps and gained no honor by taking a life. They began mutilating the bodies of army personnel they had killed as a consequence of abuse of Apache victims by white settlers.

Fear of the spirit

Most tribes performed a series of rituals after a death. Like those performed by warriors, these rituals sought to influence a departed spirit. The simplest rituals are found among the groups of the region between the Rocky Mountains and the Sierra Nevada and Cascade ranges. This region is known as the Great Basin. In this area native peoples tended to bury their dead, though more out of fear than respect. They might also bury the person's belongings with the corpse or destroy them. A dead person's possessions were never passed on.

If someone died in a dwelling, it would be abandoned. Any elderly members of the group who could no longer contribute effectively to the nomadic hunting

Scalping
Removing the skin from the head of a dead enemy, usually with its attached hair, as a battle trophy.

Curriculum Context

The practices of Apache war parties can only be fully understood in the context of the Plains economy in which they operated and the historical background of white attacks on Apache.

and gathering economy would be left to die. The point of these rituals was to place physical and mental space between the living and the dead.

Native Americans of the Northwest Coast also feared the dead. A corpse was removed from the house as quickly as possible. But it could not be taken through a regular doorway. Instead, a new makeshift opening was hacked into the wall.

In the north of the region the corpse was buried. However, in the south it was laid in a coffin box or a canoe and hung from a tree or set on branches or poles. The tribes living in the central area preferred to bury their dead.

The spirits of the dead

Most Native Americans were more fearful of a person's spirit than of his or her actual body. The Plains peoples, such as the Lakota Sioux and the Cheyenne, placed their dead on a scaffold in sacred burial grounds. First, the body was dressed in its best clothes, then wrapped in a buffalo hide. It was then put in a cradle and placed

Scaffold
In some Native American cultures, a raised platform on which the body of a dead person was left to decompose.

A print of a wood engraving by Henry François Farny, showing a Sioux warrior laid to rest on a scaffold in 1891. The favorite horse of a dead warrior was often killed and left at the foot of the scaffold.

Curriculum Context

The burial rituals undertaken by the Sioux and other Plains groups are a good example of how a culture's attitude toward nature and its religious beliefs are reflected in its practices.

in the branches of trees or on scaffolding, where it would be left to decompose. However, there was a great fear that the spirit of the dead would return to claim another life to accompany it into the spirit world. To prevent this, various precautions were taken. Since the people believed that spirits remained near corpses for a time, only close relatives went near the dead body. They often brought food and hunting weapons for the dead person to take on the journey to the spirit world.

Plains tribes also believed that displays of sorrow would help the spirit of the dead cope with the loss of his or her physical life. Women who were in mourning might trim their hair short and cut their arms and legs. Relatives might give all their belongings to the poor. If a sound was heard in the night, such as a baby crying or a wolf howling, it was feared a ghost was nearby. The family would fire guns, and a shaman would burn incense to chase the ghost away.

The next world

The Fox tribe of the Great Lakes conducted elaborate rituals after death. First there would be a night of mourning by those in the community of the same clan. Then the clan leader would speak to the corpse. He would tell the body that its duty was not to stay in the village envying the living but to journey west to the spirit world. The body might then be exposed on a scaffold or buried or cremated, depending on the final wishes of the dead person.

Fasting

Fasting is eating little or no food, and it is common practice in world religions. It was also a significant part of Native American spiritual life. Fasting was most common as a preparation for important rituals. The aim of fasting in religious ritual was to place a person in close contact with the spirit world, where there was no need to eat and drink.

Many Native Americans believed that they were made up of a body and a spirit. The body was the person in the natural world that had to have food and drink to survive, while the spirit—or lifeforce—was similar to the European idea of the soul. The spirit had an existence independent from that of the body. In order to come into contact with the spirit world, a person had to deny the body food so that their spirit could become dominant.

Fasting and bloodletting

The Aztecs and the Maya, who were ancient civilizations of Mexico, combined fasting with another form of purification known as bloodletting. They believed that blood contained great power, a power that was used by the gods who controlled their lives in order to help the natural world work, such as making sure the crops grew and the sun rose. When Aztec or Mayan priests began to fast, they would eat only one meal a day. This would usually be a bland meal of corn gruel or tortilla without any flavoring. The priests would also stab themselves in the earlobe, tongue, or thigh to draw blood that would be burned before idols of the gods.

One of the few books that has survived from the culture of ancient Mexico describes a similar ceremony of purification. It took place at the city of Tlaxcala near modern-day Mexico City. Every four years the priests

Curriculum Context

Students learning about the religious beliefs of Native American societies may be asked to focus on beliefs about the relationship between the body and spirit.

Bloodletting

The practice of removing blood from a person's body, usually in order to prevent or cure illness.

of Tlaxcala held a festival in honor of their chief god. During this festival they fasted for 80 days. At the end of the fasts they would have lost a lot of body fat, and would look skeletal, resembling a decomposing body. The purpose of this fasting was to transform the person into something like their spirit, which could only be released from the body after death.

Such extreme fasting affected the mind. When painful bloodletting rituals were combined with lack of food, and often of sleep, the mind was less able to distinguish between the physical world and an imagined or subconscious one. The person fasting experienced hallucinations, which were interpreted by the shaman (medicine man) for spiritual meaning.

The Vision Quest

Most native peoples in North and Central America believed that the spirit world could provide protection and guidance. One way spirits communicated with individuals was through visions, and Native Americans of the Plains region regularly tried to attain visions through fasting.

Vision Quest

A rite of passage in many Native American groups, in which young individuals went alone to an isolated place to seek protection from the spirits.

Many Plains tribes also used fasting as one of the elements in rites of passage, such as the initiation procedures used when a boy was ready to be a warrior. Boys going through this ritual, known as a Vision Quest, would usually go to an isolated place, often high on a hill, and wait there alone. After several days without eating, the boy would hope to have a vision or meet a spirit. It was hoped that the spirit, which might take the form of a bird or some other animal, would guide him through life.

Some people were more gifted at having visions than others. They became known as shamans and often became tribal leaders. Sitting Bull, who saw many visions during his life, was one of the most famous.

Featherwork

Featherwork is the craft of weaving or sewing together feathers to make anything from clothing to ornaments. Perhaps the most famous example of featherwork are the headdresses worn by Plains warriors, but Native Americans used the craft widely. Featherwork, including cotton and feather clothing and robes, was also widespread throughout the Southwest region.

The feathers of various birds, particularly birds of prey, were highly sought after. Also, certain birds were considered sacred, as they were believed to be messengers of the gods. The eagle, which was able to reach the sky but, according to some Native American mythology, had chosen to live on Earth, was much revered. Other birds, such as hawks and owls, were also honored and respected by various groups.

An ancient art

Featherwork can be traced back at least to the pre-Pueblo communities of the Anasazi and Hohokam. Later, Hopi and Zuni kachina dolls, representing ancestral spirits, were decorated with feathers, as were kachina masks.

A close-up of a feather bustle. Feather bustles made from eagle, hawk, or turkey feathers were traditionally worn by Plains peoples on the back of their dance regalia.

A wide-ranging trade

Feathers were a major commodity on the elaborate and flourishing trade networks that Native Americans used long before the arrival of European explorers. The Arawak people, whom Columbus encountered when he first arrived in the Caribbean, regularly made long voyages from their islands to Florida and Mexico. They exchanged various goods on these trips, but feathers and live parrots were among the most valuable items they carried. Feathers and other goods were important in maintaining trade and social links between many tribes throughout the Americas.

Prayer stick

A stick used by Pueblo peoples for prayers and in ceremonies. Feathers were attached to prayer sticks as offerings to the spirits.

Feather prayer sticks played an important part in Pueblo tribal ceremonies. The sticks were also placed along routes into Pueblo villages as protective devices and offerings when rituals were held. In some Pueblo rain dances the dancers would carry live snakes, stroking them with feathers to stop them from biting.

In California small feathers were often woven together to create a mosaic effect. For example, flicker or woodpecker feathers mounted on deerskin bands were used by the Hupa and the Pomo. Feather coronets and topknots, ear ornaments, and feathered belts, as well as turkey-feather skirts and mantles, were worn by Native Americans throughout central and southern California.

Collecting feathers

Many Pueblo tamed eagles and kept them in cages so the feathers could be collected. They also domesticated turkeys as a feather source and imported brightly colored macaw feathers from Mexico.

Plains peoples, however, usually captured and killed the eagles they required. The method they used was to dig a pit for the hunter to hide in and then cover it over and lay out some bait on top. When the eagle landed to eat, the hunter would pull it down into the pit and kill it with his bare hands. Feathers were so valuable that three eagles could be exchanged for a horse.

Games

Native Americans have always enjoyed a variety of recreational and competitive activities—some universally familiar, others uniquely Native American. The enjoyment starts early with a range of simple children's games. Many Native American children have considerable freedom to give their imaginations full rein, and games are often invented on the spur of the moment.

Starting young

In their younger years boys and girls play games together, with little or no separation of the sexes. Games that are popular at this age are the same ones played by children around the world, such as hobby-horse, tops, and leapfrog.

As they grow, Native American boys are encouraged to engage in boisterous games while girls are expected to be more reserved and sedate. But there is little disapproval of the girl who prefers to play rough-and-tumble or of the boy with more sedentary interests.

Popular games

The games played by today's teenage males are similar to those that have been played for centuries by their ancestors. They are fun games with serious intentions, teaching young males to be good hunters and warriors and demonstrating skill and dexterity.

The most popular of these is hoop and pole. Hoop and pole competitions are sometimes held between two teams from different bands or tribes. Today, as in the past, such competitions are usually accompanied by heavy wagers.

Various competitive ball games, including a version of lacrosse, are also popular with young men. Women's games, like those of the men, rely on skill. Snow snake,

Curriculum Context

A comparison of the games played by girls and boys in different groups may help students gain an understanding of gender roles in native societies.

Hoop and pole

A game in which a hoop with marked segments is rolled along the ground while a player attempts to hit it with a spear or arrow. Points are scored according to which segment the spear or arrow hits.

LA CROSSE.

Native Americans and white men playing lacrosse in the mid-19th century. Native American groups played lacrosse in Pre-Contact times.

in which a spear or pole is slid along winter ice—either to rest as close as possible to a marker or to travel the farthest—is a regular winter activity among women of the northern native peoples.

Old and new

Other Native American games include archery and ring and pin (also known as the cup game). In ring and pin a pointed stick or bone attached to a thong is swung and caught in a cup or in holes cut through a stick. Foot and horse racing, once the domain of the Plains peoples, are increasingly popular sports among most North American groups. Rodeos are now a regular feature at many modern powwows.

In the Inuit Olympics, teams from several communities vie with one another in demonstrations of traditional skills. One game is a form of trampolining in which a team member is thrown into the air from a stretched hide held by his teammates. Another is ear-pulling, in which two opponents with a thong looped around their right ears try to pull each other off balance. In a third game competitors try to catch a suspended morsel of food using a stick held between their teeth.

Powwow

A gathering of Native Americans, often involving feasting and dancing. The word comes from the Narragansett word *powwaw,* meaning shaman or magician.

Homes

There were many different types of traditional Native American homes, reflecting the diverse climates of the vast continent and the different lifestyles of its many peoples. In the far north, the major consideration was to keep out the cold and damp. Other groups lived in homes that suited a nomadic way of life. Settled farming peoples in the Southwest built permanent homes out of adobe.

Northern homes

In the far north, among the Inuit and Aleut, building materials were in short supply. In parts of the region there is no timber at all, but wind-packed snow could be cut into large blocks and used to construct domed igloos. The Arctic cold quickly froze the blocks together to create solid structures. In coastal parts of Inuit territory, where driftwood was available and the people hunted whales, homes had frameworks of timber or whalebone covered with sod and protected by earth embankments.

Mobile homes

In the subarctic interior of Canada, the most common form of shelter was the wigwam. Plains peoples used a similar design to make conical, skin-covered tepees. These were ideally suited for a nomadic way of life, since they could quickly be put up and taken down.

Multihousehold dwellings

Constant damp was the main problem for groups that lived in the damp forests of British Columbia and southern Alaska. Family clans also needed long, multihousehold dwellings. The solution was provided by the vast stands of straight-grained cedars in the forests. People split the trees into planks and attached them to log frameworks to make large multi-family buildings known as longhouses. Some were 100 feet (30 m) long and 50 feet (15 m) wide.

Curriculum Context

Students may wish to examine the various forms of shelter that Native Americans constructed in order to learn about how they adapted their lifestyles to the natural environment.

Wigwam

A domed dwelling consisting of a single room, formed by a frame of arched poles and covered with a roofing material such as birchbark, grass, or hides.

Iroquois groups of the eastern Woodland also lived in multi-family homes. They built large, log-framed houses similar to those of the Northwest Coast but covered them with sheets of heavy elm bark.

Large buildings housing several families were also common among the permanent settlements of the seminomadic groups along the Mississippi and Missouri rivers. These earth-lodges had log frameworks, but they were partly underground and were covered with a thick layer of earth over branches and boughs.

Open to the elements

Farther south the climate is hot and humid. In Florida the Seminole bands that lived near the Everglades needed homes that stood clear of the swampy ground and protected them from the heat. As a result they built communal platform-houses on stilts, with open sides to allow a constant flow of air. The houses, known as chickees, were reached by ladder.

Wickiups and hogans

The Southwest and the Great Basin, by contrast, are very hot and dry. However, summer evenings can be so cool as to become uncomfortable, and winter can be very cold. The way native peoples coped with these extremes of temperature depended on whether the group was nomadic or settled.

Nomadic groups used various types of home. In the Basin, where materials were limited, homes were often no more than brush shelters or windbreaks. Some Basin tribes, such as the Paiute, lived in more elaborate, conical shelters called wickiups. Similar to a wigwam, a wickiup was made by piling brush over a framework of poles. A few Apache groups—particularly the Jicarilla—adopted the skin-covered tepee, whereas the Navajo, whose lifestyle was less nomadic, built unique octagonal log-houses called hogans.

Chickee

A Seminole house built on stilts, with a log frame, open sides, and a thatched roof over a raised wooden platform. *Chickee* is the Seminole word for house.

Permanent homes

Settled farming peoples in the Southwest, such as the Hopi, built permanent homes out of adobe (sun-dried clay bricks). Called pueblos, these were multiroomed and multistoried buildings housing several hundred people. Early pueblos were often built in sheltered recesses in canyon walls, as at Mesa Verde in Colorado. Later they were often built on the tops of mesas (plateaus), mainly for protection against the Spanish.

Other types of homes

There were many other kinds of Native American homes. Wattle-and-daub—pole frameworks intertwined with branches plastered with mud—houses were popular with Southern tribes. The Sauk and Fox of the Great Lakes attached elm-bark mats to circular frameworks of logs. Grass and thatch houses were common in parts of the Plains among the Wichita and other groups.

The multistoried stone cliff dwellings at Mesa Verde in Colorado were built by a Pueblo people known as the Anasazi between 1100 and 1200 CE.

Jewelry

Jewelry making was widespread and highly developed among all Native Americans. A wide variety of materials were used, including shells, bone, seeds, animal teeth and claws, feathers, hair, bird and porcupine quills, sheet mica, and semiprecious stones. In recent times beads obtained through European trade have largely replaced quills and silver has become especially important among some Pueblo tribes.

Curriculum Context

Jewelry is a common find among archeological remains of early civilizations. Adorning the body was an important means of self expression and a display of status.

Jewelry making was an ancient craft, and countless numbers of seed and shell beads have been discovered at archeological sites together with other materials, such as intricately colored and patterned stones. These all show that jewelry and items of personal adornment were important to early Native American cultures.

The archeological evidence also suggests that many of these materials had been traded from distant regions. Spanish explorers in Florida and California noted that native women there wore little clothing but bedecked themselves with seed and shell necklaces, armbands, and other finery.

Practical uses

In addition to its decorative effect jewelery often served a practical purpose. Jewelry was seen as a valuable commodity which was used as currency in some tribes. Jewelry also had another important use. Belts of beads made from white and purple quahog shells, known as wampum belts, were woven with designs that symbolized treaties and agreements between the different peoples.

Wampum belt

A decorative belt made from small cylindrical beads made from polished shells. The belts were used for ceremonial purposes and to record important events.

Metal- and beadwork

European contact invigorated the trade in materials used for jewelry. Wampum beads, for instance, were manufactured commercially by the Dutch, and a factory producing them was still operating in New Jersey early in the 20th century. Other European goods were sought for decorative use.

One of the more significant trade items in this region was copper wire, which was highly valued by Native Americans for use in necklaces and armbands. Other trade metals were also eagerly sought. Brass kettles were among the more popular trade items. This was not for any practical function they had but because the kettles could be cut up and made into bracelets or rolled into tubular form for hair ornaments (when they were known as hair-pipes).

Metal jewelry

Some peoples, such as the Apache, used brass, tin, copper, and silver to make small metal cones hung as decorative fringes on bags and clothing. Metals and glass trade beads had a wide influence and are used in significant quantities today by modern craftworkers. Of the metals, silver is the most sought after. Although silver was not used extensively before Europeans arrived, by 1800 it was popular among the peoples of the Northeast. These tribes made their own silver ornaments after the American Revolution in 1776 closed the trade in silver brooches from Canada. The use of silver spread to the Great Lakes and from there on to the Plains.

Curriculum Context

The adoption of silver as a favored material in jewelry making is an example of how cultural and economic interaction with European settlers influenced Native American societies.

Jewelry as currency

Among the Pomo and other Californian tribes strings of clam shells, known as *kaia*, formed a currency: different lengths of strings had set values. It was the custom for Pomo women to wear kaia strings as a demonstration of status and wealth. Among Northwest Coast groups copper had a similar function. Among the Iroquois and Algonquian tribes of the Northeast, white and purple shells of the hard-shelled clam, or quahog, had a function similar to that of kaia and as currency were made into strings of set length.

Curriculum Context

As part of an investigation into the artistic heritage of a particular culture, students may find it reveaing to describe the types of jewelry preferred and the techniques and materials used to produce them.

By 1870 Navajo silversmiths in the Southwest, using techniques learned from Mexico, were hammering bracelets and earrings out of silver coins. But by 1890, because of a ban on the use of silver dollar coins, they were using Mexican pesos.

Craftworkers at Zuni pueblos learned silverworking from the Navajo, often combining silver with native turquoise. Zuni workers in their turn passed these skills on to craftworkers among the Hopi.

Glass beads

Glass beads have also had a major impact on modern Native American crafts. Beads became popular as a replacement for porcupine quills in intricate geometric and naturalistic patterns on bags, clothing, and jewelry. A huge industry has grown in which beadwork is applied to items such as keyrings and cigarette lighter cases.

A Navajo silversmith at work in 1915. Navajo, Zuni, and Hopi silverwork are still among the major craft industries of the Southwest today, and silver jewelry is made both for domestic use and to supply a thriving tourist industry.

Kachina

Kachina is a Hopi word that means "showing respect to the spirits." It is used to describe special spirit beings that the Hopi and other Pueblo peoples believe are responsible for keeping the world in order. Some kachinas are the ghosts of dead people who come back to help their families. Many, however, are very ancient and linked with important aspects of people's lives.

Kachinas can take many different forms. There are kachinas who control the growth of crops and kachina Cloud Beings who bring rain to help the crops grow. There are even kachina clowns whose main purpose is to make people laugh and to help them realize that, even when life is difficult, they should still remember all the good things they have been given to enjoy.

Kachina ceremonies

Kachinas are celebrated in elaborate ceremonies that take place in Pueblo villages from December until July. During these ceremonies masked dancers wear costumes that remind the people of what the kachinas look like. Some of these ceremonies are very sacred and take place in kivas, to which only those who have been taught the secrets of the kachinas are invited. Today even the public dances are restricted, and people who do not live in the Pueblo villages may not be allowed to see them.

Kachina dances

Kachina rituals follow closely the cycle of the farming year. Many of them take place in April in the open squares of the Pueblo villages and are meant to bring clouds and rain, to promote harmony in the universe, and to ensure health, long life, and happiness.

The kachina dances begin at the time of the winter solstice (December 21, the shortest day) and continue to be performed until the summer solstice (June 21, the longest day).

First comes Wuwuchim, when the fires of the Pueblo households are ritually relit. The dances continue with Soyal, when it is believed the kachinas return from their mountain homes to live again in the Pueblo villages. Then, in February the Powamu, or Bean Dance, marks the planting of beans that have been grown as seedlings in the kivas. The Powamu is also the time when children are given small, wooden kachina dolls. The dolls are to remind the children that the spirits are still living in the world during the six months when they do not live in the pueblos.

Finally, in late June, the Niman, or Home Dance, is held. It lasts for 16 days and is intended to ensure that the kachinas leave the pueblo with good feelings. Clowns, sometimes called Koyemsi, appear between the dances to make people laugh. Niman coincides with the early harvest, and corn, melons, and other foods are distributed to all the families in the village.

Curriculum Context

A study of the function of dance in ceremonies and rituals will help students gain an understanding of the ways in which traditional dances were shaped by a specific natural and economic context.

A Navajo dancer dressed as a kachina in 1904. Pueblo peoples such as the Navajo and Hopi believed that by wearing the mask of a kachina they actually became that kachina during the ceremony.

Kiva

A kiva is a ceremonial chamber built into the ground. It is used by Pueblo peoples of the Southwest as a meeting place for male members of different clans or groups of people claiming descent from a common ancestor. Kivas are also the places where ceremonies of the various clans take place, including rituals devoted to ancestral spirits, or kachinas.

Most Pueblo villages have several kivas dedicated to kachinas. The rituals devoted to kachinas are intended to bring health and prosperity to the community, as well as ensuring a good harvest every year. Some of these rituals are very sacred and are held in secret. Only people who have been taught the history of the kachina are allowed to witness them.

Ritual chambers

Kivas may be located at several places in a village, and each one is dedicated to the rituals of a particular clan group. Most are circular and are entered by a ladder from the roof.

Inside the kiva is an underground cellar that has a number of different levels built into it. They are the floor, seating platforms arranged around the kiva walls, the timbers supporting the roof, and the roof itself.

These four levels represent the four different worlds of Pueblo cosmology—that is, their philosophy and myths about how the universe began—and the way in which human beings climbed up through different levels out of darkness into the everyday world that we all live in.

Pueblo peoples believe that humans ascended from the underworld to the natural world, coming out at the "Earth Navel." It is represented in every kiva by the

Curriculum Context

Students may be asked to explore diverse beliefs about the origins of the universe in different Native American cultures.

A reconstruction of the Great Kiva at the Aztec Ruins National Monument in New Mexico. The kiva was built by Pueblo peoples in the 11th to 13th centuries and is large enough to hold over 100 people.

sipapu. The sipapu is at the center of the kiva, right below the ladder, and is therefore considered to be extremely important. The actual location of the Earth's navel is uncertain, but most Pueblo groups believe it might be an unidentified badger hole somewhere in the San Francisco Mountains.

Great kivas

Although modern kivas are associated with specific Pueblo villages, archeological studies suggest there may have been great kivas in the past that served the needs of people from a much wider area. One of them has been found at Aztec Ruins in New Mexico. Experts believe that the size of Aztec Ruins shows that this kiva and other great kivas probably served as ceremonial centers for large numbers of people living apart from one another.

Lacrosse

Lacrosse, adopted as the national game of Canada in 1859, originated in Pre-Contact times with Algonquian and Iroquoian tribes of the Atlantic seaboard. It was later played in the Great Lakes area, the Midwest, and parts of the Northwest Coast and California. The principle of the game, which is to throw a ball between goalposts using a racquet, has remained unchanged.

However, the modern version played by 10 players on each side between goals 80 yards (73 m) apart is a tame version of the original. The first white observers were astonished by the numbers of participants, up to 600 on each team, and the immensity of the playing fields: goalposts might be 1 mile (1.6 km) apart.

The vigor with which the game was played was also cause for comment. Little heed was paid to safety of life or limb or to ensuring that the rules were followed precisely. Observers noted the game was played with such speed and violence it seemed as if the teams were warring nations rather than rival ballteams. In some respects these comments were more accurate than their makers may have realized, since the Iroquois considered lacrosse a training exercise for war.

Preparatory rites

Players underwent lengthy preparatory rites conducted by shamans (medicine men). One rite was intended to prevent players eating rabbit or frog. The rabbit is timid, while the frog's bones are easily broken. It was believed that eating those animals made the players vulnerable in the same ways. The ritual preparation reflects the mythical origins of the first lacrosse game. Native Americans believed it took place between the birds and animals. The bat and flying squirrel won the game for the birds and acquired supernatural power.

Curriculum Context

The ritual preparation that lacrosse players underwent is a good example of a traditional practice that reflects the attitude of Native Americans toward nature.

Literature

The Cherokee invented an alphabet in the 19th century, the Inuit and Cree have their own writing systems, and the Navajo and Sioux today translate their spoken language into Western alphabetical writing systems. Yet these are not the only ways that native North Americans have communicated their knowledge to others.

Curriculum Context

Many curricula emphasize the importance of enriching the study of history by reading fiction and poems to help understand the lives of the people being studied.

For centuries Native American tales and stories have been told orally (one person talking to others). Many of those stories are now preserved in written form. A written literary tradition is fairly recent for Native Americans. This is partly because they mistrusted the American education system, and also because white Americans often thought that Native Americans had nothing to contribute to the national culture.

Life stories

Books about Native American stories and experiences written by Native Americans began to be published between 1890 and 1930. Many of these books became popular when white people found it interesting to read about the lives and experiences of Native Americans written in their own words.

Curriculum Context

Autobiographical works by writers such as Gerald Vizenor and Francis La Flesche help students understand the values and ideas of people in Native American societies.

Nancy Lurie's *Mountain Wolf Woman*, which tells the life story of a Winnebago Native American, and John Neihardt's *Black Elk Speaks* are two particular examples of the 20th-century trend in literature. Other famous non-fiction accounts or memoirs include *Lame Deer, Seeker of Visions* by J. Erdoes; the more recent *Interior Landscapes*, written by the world-famous Gerald Vizenor, a Chippewa; and Omaha Francis La Flesche's book *The Middle Five,* an early account of his days in a Nebraska mission school. *Indian Boyhood* by Charles Eastman, a Sioux, and the fictionalized *Waterlily* by Ella Deloria, also a Sioux, published in 1988, have both been very widely read. Scott Momaday, a Kiowa who won the prestigious Pulitzer Prize with his *House Made of Dawn* in 1968, is one of the most published Native American writers today.

The richness of the Native American oral tradition before books were introduced is also expressed in the printed texts of the speeches of tribal orators such as Deskaheh (Iroquois) and Chief Joseph's last speech.

Tricksters and reservations

The development of Native American literature has also been affected by different writers choosing particular themes and ideas from traditional Native American culture.

The Trickster is one example of the traditional figures used in modern Native American literature. It is the favorite subject of Vizenor and the Cherokee Thomas King. Community and family life are discussed in *Love Medicine*, by Louise Erdrich (Ojibway) and in many works by native poets such as Simon Ortiz (Acoma), Linda Hogan (Chickasaw), Lance Henson (Cheyenne), Luci Tapahonso (Navajo), Beth Brant (Mohawk), and Paula Gunn Allen (Laguna).

Fiction writing

Representations of Native Americans in fiction have more recently expressed touching images of reservation life or feelings about being Native American in a largely white American society. These are the themes of *Winter in the Blood* (1975) by James Welch of the Blackfoot-Gros Ventre and *Ceremony* (1977) by Leslie Marmon Silko of the Laguna.

Native American literature today also deals openly with political issues. Sioux writer Vine Deloria in her book *Custer Died for Your Sins*, Cherokee writer and artist Jimmie Durham, and the controversial

Menominee poet, Christos, have all addressed Native American political themes in their work.

Myth and reality

Many familiar stereotypes of Native Americans are the product of white literature and films. The way in which Native Americans have been treated in books has changed a lot from the early images of the "Vanishing Indian" portrayed in James Fenimore Cooper's *The Last of the Mohicans*. Native Americans were often represented negatively in Hollywood films, and this has also changed in the last 20 years.

When they were not represented negatively, Native Americans were treated as heroes for children's entertainment, such as in Henry Wadsworth Longfellow's *Hiawatha*, or as silent figures existing in a world that the Native American character could never be a part of, such as Tashtego in Herman Melville's *Moby Dick*.

The fascination with Native American cultures can also be found in the works of such world-famous writers as D. H. Lawrence, whose interest in Central American mythology lies behind such books as *The Plumed Serpent*.

Modern books have continued to produce images of Native Americans as figures of the past, such as in the bestseller *Hanta Yo* by Ruth Beebe Hill (1979). In recent years, however, there has been an effort to represent Native Americans in a realistic and less romantic way.

Curriculum Context

When reading works of fiction such as Longfellow's *Hiawatha* and Melville's *Moby Dick*, students may be asked to consider whether the books represent Native American cultures in a realistic way.

Longhouse Religion

Longhouse religion is the traditional Iroquois religion. Still practiced today, it has changed to help the Iroquois fit into a world dominated by people from European cultures. It was founded following a vision of the Iroquois chief Handsome Lake in 1799, at a time when white settlement in western New York State was pushing the Iroquois off their homeland.

Handsome Lake (1735–1815) was a leading Iroquois chief, or sachem. In 1799 he suffered a severe illness. While he was sick, he experienced a vision that showed him that the Iroquois would have to alter many of their traditional practices if they were to survive.

Lifestyle changes

Handsome Lake was a devout Christian who tried to blend Iroquois beliefs with Christianity. His reforms demanded the Iroquois had to live in families based on a married couple and their children.

The Iroquois became converted to the ideas of Handsome Lake and began to put them into practice. He said that the "medicine societies," which were the focus of Iroquois religious life, must reduce their influence. After Handsome Lake's death the medicine societies regained some influence, but most of his reforms remained in force. The result was the Longhouse religion as it is now practiced.

Rituals and festivals

The cycle of ceremonies in Longhouse religion follows the pattern of the agricultural year. The midwinter festival, a ritual lasting eight days, marks both the end of the old cycle, when things have stopped growing, and the beginning of a new one, when growth returns. During the first four days, rituals emphasize the passing of the old year. Ashes are cleared from fire pits, people confess their sins, and the False Face Society performs rituals to cure the sick and help those suffering from bad luck. The next four days see sacred rituals that welcome the hope of the new year—the Feather Dance, the Skin or Drum Dance, chanting, and a game of bowling. There is also a tobacco ritual that asks all spirits to bless people during the coming year. Other ceremonies that follow during the year include the Bush Dance, the Thanks-to-the-Maple ritual, and the Green Corn festival.

Eight societies

Festivals and ceremonies are performed by eight ritual societies. The Society of Medicine Men, also known as the Shake the Pumpkin society, is the largest. All the members of the other seven societies are automatically members of the Medicine Men.

The Medicine Men deal with matters of health and luck. The Company of Mystic Animals celebrates the spirits of the natural world, while the Little Water Medicine Society controls the most power and was linked to warfare. The Little People or Dark Dance Society fosters a good rapport with supernatural imps who can be helpful or mischievous, and the False Face Society cleanses the Iroquois of disease in spring and fall, using ritual masks to communicate with the spirits.

The Husk Face Society is an agricultural group that performs a dance at midwinter, representing the return of the crops for the coming planting. The Towii'sas is an all-woman society that honors the three basic crops of the Iroquois—corn, beans, and squash. Finally, the Ohigwe Society maintains the boundary between the worlds of the dead and the living.

Marriage

Traditional American marriages often appeared strange to Western eyes, since they were not bound by Christian conventions and rules. For all native peoples marriage was a bond between two extended families as well as between two individuals. For the Cheyenne and Arapaho a marriage was the single most important event in a person's life.

Because of their significance, traditional Native American marriages were subject to strict rules. The most important rule was that blood relatives, even quite distant ones, were not allowed to marry. This rule was often extended to include persons who were not related by blood but who belonged to the same clan or to a related clan. Among the Tlingit marriage was forbidden to anyone, even to members of other tribes, who claimed descent from the same mythical ancestor.

The importance of virtue

Such restrictions meant that often prospective marriage partners could meet only at annual gatherings, when several families and clans camped

Curriculum Context

A comparison of the significance of marriage in different groups helps students gain a deeper understanding of the social organization of various peoples.

Charging Thunder and his wife, members of the Sioux, photographed in about 1900. In most Native American groups, marriage between two people was intended to last for the rest of their lives.

together for tribal ceremonies. At such times young, sexually mature women were closely chaperoned, since among most tribes it was essential they remain chaste until marriage.

A marriage was usually arranged by the relatives of the prospective bride and groom. A woman's brother often decided whom she might marry, but it was usual to take a couple's preferences into account, for it was believed that forced marriages were unlikely to last or be happy.

Parents were always concerned that their children should marry well, within their own class and to someone of similar status—although there were exceptions to this last rule—and that the marriage should be an honorable one. Elopements sometimes occurred—young couples secretly left a camp to live together. Such relationships did not have the blessing or approval of arranged marriages, but if they proved stable, they were generally accepted, and the couples lost no status or respect.

In many Native American groups a man could not marry until he had proved himself. For example, a Micmac man could not marry until he had spent up to two years living and working with his prospective father-in-law. During this time he had to prove his skills as a provider and hunter. Similarly, a Comanche man had to prove himself as a hunter and a warrior before he could marry. For this reason few Native American men married until they were in their twenties, while most Native American women could marry as soon as they were sexually mature.

Exchange of gifts
In the case of an arranged marriage relatives of the man or woman—after lengthy family discussion—sent a representative to the other family with gifts. Which

Curriculum Context

In anthropological studies of different cultures, students may choose to examine how gender roles are reflected in Native American marriage practices.

family made the first move varied from tribe to tribe, but it was usually the man's. The family representative made a speech extolling the man's virtues, and if the gifts were accepted, then the marriage arrangements went ahead.

Most families thought of the gifts—horses and weapons for the men, clothing, robes, and drygoods for the women—as an honorable demonstration of the man's potential as a provider and not as an attempt to "buy" a wife. Later, gifts of equal or greater value would be given by the woman's relatives in honor of their own family name.

Family ties

The young couple then started living together as husband and wife with one of the families. If the couple lived with the wife's family, it became the son-in-law's responsibility to care and provide for his wife's older relatives.

Marriages and the family ties they established were intended to last for life, but couples could divorce if they wanted to. In the case of a couple living with the wife's family, the woman owned all the household items and when choosing to end a marriage placed her husband's few belongings outside to indicate that he was no longer welcome. If the married couple were living with the husband's family, the wife returned to her family. In nearly all cases of divorce, young children remained with their mother.

In some native peoples, such as the Comanche, polygamy—a man having more than one wife—was common. Usually, however, a man could marry only as many wives as he could afford to provide for. For this reason polygamy was practiced mainly by tribal chiefs and other rich men.

Masks

Many Native Americans used masks in their religious rituals and ceremonies. The masks were made from a variety of different materials and were often painted with designs representing a spirit or ancestor. Many masks were made for specific tribal rituals or ceremonies, during which the presence of the mask played an essential role and symbolized the connection between the human and spirit worlds.

Curriculum Context

The use of masks to provide a link between the living and the dead in Native American societies is a good example of how beliefs about the natural and supernatural worlds are reflected in customs and artistic output.

A link to the spirit world

In traditional cultures the spirit world is as real as the natural world. Masks served to provide a link between these two worlds and also reminded native peoples that the supernatural beings were available to give them help and assistance. Many of these connections were explained in tribal stories and legends, which were told during the winter months.

Different groups used masks in different ways. For example, the Iroquois tribe members who wore Husk Faces went from longhouse to longhouse performing a dance that represented the return of the crops in the spring. Another example of masks being used in rituals to ask favors of the spirits was the Kachina Dance of the Hopi. This, too, was performed in the hope of a successful harvest.

The Kwakiutl used masks in their Hamatsa Dance to commemorate an important supernatural event in their folklore. The dance was an initiation ceremony for new members of the community. The dancer represented a tribal ancestor who changed from a human to a spirit and learned some of the dances of the spirit world. The ancestor then returned to the group, where more ritual dances made him human again. He then taught other members of the group the spirit dances he had learned.

More than just symbolic

During such rituals it was believed the performers did not just play the roles of the spirits depicted by their masks. The masks helped the dancers actually become the spirits that they were portraying for the duration of the dance.

For example, when a group of Hopi villagers watched the dance to celebrate the kachinas (ancestral spirits), they believed that they were not just watching their masked neighbors perform a dance but were seeing them change before their very eyes into the kachina that made successful farming possible.

In this way the mask helped create a powerful social bond between people. If people believed their neighbor played an important part in the successful growing of their crops, they were much more likely to treat him or her, and their community, with respect.

Zahadolzha, a Navajo, wearing a leather mask in 1904. The Navajo and other Pueblo peoples used masks in elaborate healing rituals and dances celebrating their ancestral spirits.

Carved masks

Since masks were considered to be so important, great care went into making them. For example, Iroquois mask carvers went into the forest to look for the right tree—preferably a basswood, cucumber, or willow tree. The carver worked into the tree, carving the face into the living wood. He then carefully removed the mask in one piece and smoothed and polished the inside. If he carved the mask in the morning, he painted it red. If he carved it in the afternoon or evening, he painted it black.

Sometimes masks also acquired other social meanings. On the Northwest Coast they were owned by individual families. Since some of the masks were used only in the important dances, they would show the status of the dancer and the dancer's family when they were worn.

Mask styles

Masks were usually stylized and always showed specific features. The False Face masks of the Iroquois all had twisted noses because, according to legend, the giant False Face ran into a mountain and broke his nose. The Haida people made masks of the Cannibal Spirit in two separate halves. At a specific point in the dance the two halves opened to reveal the face of the dancer, who represented a human prisoner of the spirit.

Caring for masks

Native American masks often belonged to specific ritual or religious groups and might be looked after by people who had a special duty to care for them. In Pueblo communities, the masks that were used in the dances to celebrate the kachinas (ancestral spirits) were kept in the sacred ritual centers called kivas, where they were guarded by kiva priests. The Iroquois covered their False Face masks with hide or cloth and hung them so that they faced the wall. In this way the power of the False Face masks was concealed and kept pure until the masks were taken down and used again.

Curriculum Context

Students may be asked to investigate specific features of masks that reflect their purpose. The False Face masks of the Iroquois and Haida masks representing the Cannibal Spirit are good examples.

Medicine Bundle

Medicine bundles were collections of objects normally kept in a pouch made from an animal or bird skin. The bundles acted as symbols linking the person who made or owned the bundle to the animal spirits who appeared in the person's vision, which gave the owner special power. The bundles could bring the owner success in battle or hunting, or benefit the whole community.

The power of the bundle

Native Americans believed in many gods and spirits. These spirits became visible to individuals during intense dreams or visions, giving them power that could be used to do good and counteract evil. Such power could be used to cure an illness or bring a person good luck.

During the vision the animal spirit instructed the person having the vision to make a medicine bundle that was somehow associated with the animal. In other words, if a man dreamed of a beaver, then he would use a beaver skin for his bundle. The bundles also contained other objects, such as rocks, beads, animal claws, or parts of plants.

Anyone could own a medicine bundle, providing the person had had a vision explaining its use. Although the bundles themselves did not possess any power, they reminded their owners of the original visions or dreams and could therefore be used to reactivate them during ceremonies.

Tribal bundles

Medicine bundles figured in mythical accounts of the past. The Navajo believed that a medicine bundle brought from the underworld was used by First Man and First Woman in an all-night ceremony at the Place of Emergence to set in place the "inner forms" of the

Curriculum Context

Students learning about religious practices and folklore in Native American societies should be aware how the use of medicine bundles reflects broader beliefs.

Medicine bundles contained items that would link the owner to the spirit world but in a way only the owner would understand.

natural world. This bundle was passed on to Changing Woman, who used it to create corn. Thus the power of a medicine bundle could start life itself.

Some bundles belonged to sacred societies. The bundle of a society often included an object that the society believed once belonged to an early ancestor. The Iroquois had eight ritual societies that used medicine bundles. The most powerful of them was the Little Water Medicine, which used a special potion made from water and animal parts with its bundles.

The Pawnee made bundles from animal hide, which they painted with patterns to represent stars. Sometimes they wrapped the hide around an ear of corn to unite the animal world with that of agriculture. The Pawnee were both hunters and farmers, and this helped ensure a yearly supply of food.

Medicine Wheel

The medicine wheel, or sacred circle, was a common Native American symbol. In some places it was a sign for healing, but it could also be a representation of the four seasons or the four stages of human life—childhood, adolescence, maturity, and old age. It was often painted on rocks and war shields. Giant medicine wheels were also marked out with stones on hills and mountains.

Symbol of the universe

A medicine wheel is a form of mandala that represents the world and the surrounding forces of the universe. The outer circle symbolizes the edge of the world, while the spokes of the wheel cross the center and represent the sacred paths of the sun and of humanity. An altar at the center, which was sometimes marked with an eagle feather or a buffalo skull, stands for the power of the Creator.

Mandala

A circular design representing the universe.

Mountain wheel

The largest medicine wheel in the United States was built atop the west peak of Medicine Mountain in Bighorn National Forest, Wyoming. Made up of limestone slabs and boulders, it is 75 feet (23 m) wide and has a circumference of 245 feet (74 m). At the center is a circular mound 3 feet (1 m) high, which probably represents the sun. Radiating from this central mound are 28 long, narrow spokes, which may relate to the 28 days of the lunar month. Several low shelters were built at varying distances from the center. These may have represented the planets and their different positions in relation to the sun.

The exact meaning of the medicine wheel at Bighorn is unknown. The Crow, who live in the area, say it is ancient but have no myths or legends to explain its origin. It is seen by them as a place of mystery.

Curriculum Context

The medicine wheel in the Bighorn National Forest is a good example of a physical structure that can be interpreted in order to understand Native American beliefs about the nature of the universe.

Music

In many Native American myths the Creator sang things into being and then provided them with a natural song: the sighing of the wind, the mating cries of birds, the laughter of a bubbling brook, the steady rhythm of waves breaking on the shore. In traditional native music, therefore, natural songs and rhythms predominate.

Curriculum Context

The distinguishing characteristics of musical styles from different groups are an important part of understanding the historical and cultural dimensions of music.

A Kwakiutl song from the Northwest Coast, with its sharp and powerful rhythm, repeats the rhythmic pounding of the waves, while its melody echoes the cries of seagulls and the calls of ancestors. Similarly, when the Hopi Dawnlight-Youths and Butterfly-Maidens sang the *Hevebe Tawi*—songs for rain—their chanting and joyous clapping repeated the steady patter of rain sent by the Cloud God.

Songs form the basis of most Native American music, but singing was usually accompanied by percussion instruments, such as drums, clappers, rasps, and rattles.

Peoples of the Northwest Coast used painted box-drums made from wood and suspended from ceiling beams, while Pueblo people of the Southwest used drums that were hollowed-out sections of large logs. The water drums of the Woodland Ojibway (Chippewa) and Iroquois had plugs to change the level of water inside and so alter their tone.

Natural materials
Other percussion instruments had similar characteristics but varied in detail. Northwest Coast rattles were made from wood, ones from the Plains from rawhide, and those used in the Southeast and Southwest from hollowed-out gourds. Iroquois rattles were made from the shells of small turtles and filled with pebbles or dried seeds. Rasps were made from notched wood or the

notched spine of a deer's shoulder blade—rubbing sticks along them produced the rasping sound.

Apache violins

The Apache were unique in using a one-string fiddle, which they copied from Mexican violins. This has given rise to the present-day use of violins in Matachines dances in the Southwest, combining Native American and Spanish elements.

Wind instruments

Small bone tubes with a hole near the center were used as bird calls by Pueblo peoples, while people of the Great Lakes used rolled birchbark trumpets to imitate bellowing moose. Long bird-bones were often used for double flutes and dance whistles. End-flutes, which produced a haunting sound, were used by men of Plains and Great Lakes groups for playing love songs on hillsides in the evening.

In many Native American groups the flute was used as a courting instrument and to produce music for ritual dances and ceremonies. This photograph, taken in 1870, shows a member of the Yuma tribe of Arizona playing a flute made from cane.

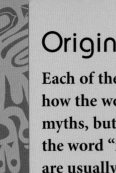

Origin Myths

Each of the Native American groups had a story that describes how the world began. These stories are sometimes called origin myths, but they are also known as sacred origin histories because the word "myth" suggests that something is not true. Origin myths are usually used by Native American groups to explain the way in which a particular tribal community came to be organized.

Curriculum Context

A knowledge of explanations given by Native American groups for the origin of the universe and humankind can help to explain the reaction of different groups to historical events.

The first beings

The most important figures in origin myths are those known as the First Beings. Even if these beings were regarded as human, they were honored as supernatural or spiritual because they were the very first beings to be created. The Iroquois, for example, believe in the Sky Woman, who came down from the sky world into the middle world. Therefore, for the Iroquois, the Sky Woman is not just human but almost a god.

The Navajo believe in an original human couple, First Man and First Woman. They came out of the underworld and created the boundaries of the Navajo world by placing the stars in the sky and building up the mountains from earth and stones.

The Yurok of northern California believe in a being called Worldmaker. This figure created the sky using pieces of rope tied together like a net. Worldmaker threw the net up into the air, where it stuck and became the sky. The ends of the net were weighed down at the edge of the ocean, but the net was able to rise and fall. As it fell, it would splash into the ocean and make the waves that wash the shore.

Curriculum Context

The origin histories of the Yurok are a good example of how Native American beliefs are influenced by the natural environment.

This story shows how origin histories reflect the habitat of a people. The Yurok live along the Pacific coast, and fish is a very important part of their diet. Every Yurok community would be familiar with the weighted nets that they tossed over the sides of their canoes for fish. The stars could be thought of as the light of heaven showing through the net's holes.

Mayan religion

The Maya dominated the Yucatán Peninsula in Mexico in Pre-Contact times. In the Mayan holy book called the *Popol Vuh* there is an account of two gods who began talking to one another over a still sea. Simply by speaking about the Earth and mountains, the two gods brought them up out of the sea. They then placed animals on the Earth.

Human beings were created to satisfy the gods' desire to be worshiped. However, humans could think and reason, and this frightened the gods so much that they limited humans' ability to see. In this way humans, would always have to rely on the gods' favor. To gain this favor, the Maya believed they must sacrifice other human beings so that the hearts and blood of the victims could be used to feed the gods.

This massive stone column in Canyon de Chelly, Arizona, is known as Spider Rock. It is believed to be the home of Na'ashje'i Asdzau, or Spider Woman, an important god in the creation stories of the Navajo people.

Potlatch

The word "potlatch" comes from the Chinook word *patshatl*, meaning "give away," and describes a social and religious custom of the Northwest Coast peoples. A potlatch is a gift-giving ceremony usually held at important points in a person's life or in a family's history. These include the building of a new house, the erecting of a totem pole, marriage, or coming of age.

Curriculum Context

Potlatches are a good example of rituals that show the importance of family as a social unit in Native American societies.

A potlatch is also held when ownership of names, dances, songs, and ceremonial costumes and masks is passed on. In the 19th century the potlatch became a means of challenging the status of a rival family.

Whatever the reason for holding a potlatch, it always includes ritual speeches, songs, and dances that demonstrate why the hosts are entitled to claim the privileges they say are theirs. By accepting the gifts, the tribe members show that they approve of the host's increase in status or other life change.

Different potlatches

Potlatches vary in size depending on the importance of the occasion and the wealth of the family involved. A poor family, for example, might invite a few close relatives to their daughter's ear-piercing and naming ceremony. But a rich family celebrating, for example, their son's inheritance of a prestigious position in a chief's household might invite people from villages many miles away. Guests for such a potlatch might number several hundred, and preparations for the event could begin years in advance.

Curriculum Context

Students may be asked to explore the importance of family organization in different cultures and examine how family ties affect the social structure of a society.

In the past important potlatches were held during *tsetseka*, the sacred winter season, when the people's time was not taken up with hunting or gathering food, therefore enabling them to attend ceremonies that could last several days.

Kaw-Claa, a member of the Tlingit from the Northwest Coast, photographed in 1906 in full potlatch dancing costume.

Links to the spirit world

During a potlatch, stories of the hosts' ancestors are recited to explain how the hosts' forebears rose to prominence in the tribe. Like many Native Americans, Northwest Coast peoples believe that all humans can gain status, power, and wealth through supernatural intervention. By reciting these stories and handing out gifts, the hosts acknowledge the family's debt to their esteemed ancestors and ask for the spirits' continued intervention.

The food consumed and gifts distributed at a potlatch serve as links to the supernatural world. People might eat massive quantities of dried salmon, and this would be seen as showing respect and thanks to the Great Salmon, the divine spirit of the fish. However, such excessive feasting at a potlatch could also be a demonstration, for example, of a wealthy family's ownership of productive salmon-fishing grounds.

Curriculum Context

Students learning about the central religious beliefs of native peoples may wish to highlight the influence of the supernatural world in the organization of some societies.

Valuable copper plaques are sometimes given away during a potlatch. They are said to be the temporary homes of captured souls who await reincarnation. The family receiving the plaques was obliged to give gifts of even greater value in order to retain its own tribal status. Also, the dishes in which the food is served, which are thought of as resting places for the animals who have sacrificed themselves to make the potlatch possible, might be presented as gifts.

Rivalry

In the 19th century the potlatch was increasingly used as a way of shaming a rival. Families used a potlatch to validate a position of social importance they knew a rival family might challenge. By attending the potlatch and accepting the gifts, the rivals recognized the reality of the situation and could regain status only by elevating one of their own family members to an even higher position. To do so, they held a more lavish potlatch. To refuse an invitation was regarded as socially unacceptable and would be considered an admission of defeat and imply that the rivals did not have the wealth to hold a bigger potlatch.

Curriculum Context

Students may be asked to examine the reasons for the development of 19th-century Indian policy in the United States and Canada and evaluate its legacy.

Forbidden potlatches

The Canadian government banned the potlatch in 1876 because it was seen as reinforcing native ideals and preventing the acceptance of Western values. However, tribes continued to hold them in secret because of the pressure to maintain social position. There was also a belief that if potlatches were not held, the ancestral spirits would become angry and chaos would overwhelm the world.

The government ban on the potlatch was finally lifted in 1951. Although the potlatch is again an important means of restating the people's links with the past and their ancestors, it is increasingly valued today as a way of reinforcing tribal identity and unity.

Pyramids

Pyramids and pyramid-shaped temple mounds are found in North, Central, and South America, as well as in the Southeast and Woodland regions of the United States. They are scattered over a vast area. Little is known about the connections between the different sites, but scholars understand a great deal about the people who used to live in these different places.

Many of the pyramids are huge. Some are as high as 100 feet (30 m), and the groundplan of the massive Monks Mound at Cahokia, east of St. Louis, is 1,040 feet (316 m) long by 790 feet (241 m) wide. To carry the earth and rubble used to form the core of such a pyramid would have been an immense undertaking. The pyramid must, therefore, have been built by highly organized teams of laborers.

Organization of such a workforce was in the hands of skilled architects, and they in turn were instructed by priests and the ruling nobility who ordered the works to be done and used tax income to finance the

The Pyramid of the Sun at Teotihuacan, Mexico. Teotihuacán was the first true city in Mesoamerica. At its peak about 600 CE more than 100,000 people lived there.

Curriculum Context

Students may be asked to trace the rise of hierarchical societies and explain their social and economic organization and political structures.

Curriculum Context

In a study of major Pre-Contact settlements, students may be required to describe what distinctive structures reveal about the beliefs of the civilizations that constructed them.

building. These societies must have been hierarchies ruled by wealthy families, whose remains are sometimes found buried in chambers in the pyramids.

Why pyramids were built

The reasons for building the pyramids varied. Sometimes they were dedicated to the gods, such as the Pyramid of the Sun and the Pyramid of the Moon at Teotihuacán near present-day Mexico City. The Temple of the Niches at El Tajín, Veracruz, had calendrical and astronomical significance.

Whatever the reason for building an individual pyramid, all of them were parts of large complexes in which several pyramids, other temples, courtyards, and plazas served as communal centers for smaller, outlying communities. People who lived and farmed in the vicinity of a pyramid complex would make regular visits for the many ceremonies that took place throughout the year.

People also used the centers as trading markets for their goods. For these reasons most of the pyramid sites are located on trade routes.

The dates at which the pyramids were built vary from as early as 15,000 BCE to about 700 CE. Almost all the pyramid complexes had been abandoned by the time they were first seen by Europeans.

Warfare, changes in political power, disease, or even overpopulation may all have contributed to the reasons for abandonment. Modern archeologists, working with teams of experts from other disciplines, are only now beginning to piece together the intricate details that will reveal even more about the lives of the Native American pyramid builders.

Quillwork and Beadwork

The craft of decorating clothing and other personal objects using porcupine quills is unique to native peoples. Quillwork was originally developed in the Subarctic and Woodland regions, and spread from there to tribes living on the Northwest Coast and the Great Plains. As European trade patterns developed, quills were gradually replaced by glass beads.

Quillwork techniques

Porcupine quills, which can grow to as long as 5 inches (12.5 cm), become soft and flexible when wet and can be colored with plant and mineral dyes. In the most frequently used quillwork technique, softened and dyed quills were wrapped or folded around a sinew thread, which was then sewn onto cloth or dried animal skin. The most delicate quillwork was tightly woven, giving the impression of many rows of small cylindrical beads.

Styles from Europe

Early European influence altered some forms of traditional quillwork. The modern styles of Huron

A detail of a Potawatomi beaded bag. The Potawatomi were highly skilled in both quillwork and beadwork. Traditionally they made beads from small shells or pieces of bone, but after the arrival of the Europeans they used imported glass beads.

and Iroquois embroidery, which combine quills with moose hair, were probably copied from the embroidery of the first French settlers. Beginning in the 17th century, the Micmac of Newfoundland applied quill decoration to birchbark boxes and other goods that they sold to European settlers.

The use of glass beads

The use of imported glass beads began in the eastern Woodland regions about 1675 and spread to all other quillworking areas. The use of beads made it unnecessary to go through the processes of softening and dyeing quills, and large areas could be covered more quickly. This made beads ideal for decorative panels on clothing, blankets, bags, and other articles.

Plains beadwork

The area best known for beadwork is the Plains, where lazy-stitch, in which beads are sewn in short rows fastened only at the ends, is the most popular style. With this technique, large areas could be rapidly covered. Many Sioux dresses feature fine beadwork with a heavily beaded capelike collar that reaches to the shoulders.

Early Plains beadwork used large pony beads, readily available through trade from 1800. The designs were mostly geometric, following patterns used in quillworking. Work from 1860 until the present generally uses smaller seed beads.

Quillwork and beadwork today

Few people now practice the craft of quillwork. However, beadworking sold to tourists and among Native Americans remains a major source of income for many traditional craftworkers today.

Curriculum Context

The increased use of imported glass beads rather than quills is a good example of the effects of cultural and economic interaction between Native Americans and European settlers.

Curriculum Context

Students may be asked to describe how cultures have been transformed by forces of modernization while retaining aspects of their cultural heritage.

Ritual

All cultures have rituals, which are symbolic acts or gestures that follow set patterns and determine how a ceremony will be conducted. Native Americans have two types of ritual—public and private. Both use a combination of some, or all, of face- and body-painting, dance, songs and chants, music played on drums or rattles, and dramatic impersonations of the gods.

Rituals are the structure or procedures of a ceremony. It is believed by many cultures that if the procedures of a ceremony are performed correctly, the desired effect will occur. In Christianity, for example, it is believed that the ritual of baptism will ensure that the baptized person will go to heaven when he or she dies.

Curriculum Context

A study of the purpose of ceremonial rituals in different societies is key to understanding the cultural and religious traditions of different societies.

Tribal or group ceremonies

Public rituals usually mark events of importance for the whole community and the entire community may become involved as either performers or spectators. Such rituals are often meant to bring general blessings for everyone. The Iroquois, for example, start their agricultural year with the Midwinter Festival in which everyone participates. During the festival dancers

Members of the Arikara, a Plains people of the Upper Missouri region, perform a medicine ceremony in 1908. Rituals of this kind played an important part in the group's religious life.

Curriculum Context

Iroquois festivals are a
good example of how
Native American societies
expressed their beliefs
and culture in rituals,
music, and dance.

perform a ritual journey that represents the one made
by the spirit forces of corn returning from their winter
homes to the Iroquois fields.

A Teton Sioux,
Picket Pin,
photographed
in 1907 holding the
skull of a buffalo
as part of the Hy
Kalowa Pi ceremony.
Buffalo were an
essential part of life
for the Plains
peoples and played
an important role in
many rituals.

The Hopi of the Southwest have a similar ceremony,
called Powamuy, for planting crops of beans. During
Powamuy bean seedlings that have been grown in
the kivas (underground ceremonial chambers) and
cultivated by Hopi priests, who would have used
special chants to ensure strong growth, are brought
out into the public plaza of the village, where the
whole community has gathered. Masked dancers who
represent the kachinas (ancestral spirits that safeguard
the Hopi) distribute the bean seedlings among all the
people, who will plant them.

Other rituals conducted for an individual were only semipublic. Fewer people witnessed such rituals because essential parts of the ritual were often carried out secretly. The Apache puberty ritual for girls is a combination of semiprivate and public ceremonies. First, the adolescent girl is accompanied by her mother and an older female attendant of the tribe who directs the secret ritual procedures. This is followed by a public ceremony in which the girl is believed to be possessed by the healing power of White Painted Woman, and other tribal members come to her for her blessing.

Rituals for the individual

Private rituals often involve only the individual and an instructor, usually a shaman (medicine man or woman) who ensures that the procedures are carried out correctly. In the Vision Quests undertaken by many Native American boys (and some girls) to obtain a personal spirit guide or helper, it is important that ritual details are followed closely. The youth must first undertake purification in a sweat lodge that has been ritually cleansed by a shaman. Then, on his own, the youth goes without food and water for a period of four days in some isolated place. During this stage he hopes to receive a dream, or vision, in which he will be given guidelines by the spirits about how to conduct his life.

Sweat lodge
A steam-filled shelter used in ceremonies performed to make contact with the spirits.

If the procedures of the ritual have not been followed properly, however, then the vision will be a negative one: the boy will either receive no help or guidance, or the guidance will be given only on condition that he lives according to strict taboos.

In all Native American rituals there is an emphasis on contacts with the spirit world and on gaining a greater sense of spiritual awareness. This is because all Native American rituals are ultimately intended to maintain harmony between people and sacred beings.

Sand Paintings

The Navajo of the Southwest make sand paintings as part of healing ceremonies conducted by shamans—medicine men and women. The painters trickle finely-ground colored powders through their fingers onto cleaned, flat sand to create designs representing aspects from Navajo legends. The colored powders come from a number of sources, each of sacred significance.

Sacred Beings
In Navajo religion, spiritual beings who created humans.

Hogan
A traditional Navajo dwelling and site of religious ceremonies. The Navajo believe that hogans are one of the most sacred places, binding the people to their land.

The main colors of powder used—yellow, red, white, and black—relate to the four directions in which the Sacred Beings live. By using these materials to represent the legends, the Navajo believe that a sand painting incorporates the essence, or essential quality, of the Sacred Beings themselves.

The Navajo make sand paintings as blessings to ask for good health, long life, and happiness by ensuring there is harmony between people, nature, and the spiritual world. They make them when someone falls ill, so as to transfer the illness to the sand painting itself. At the end of the ceremony, they take the colored sand into the desert and bury it to carry the ill omens away from the homes of the Navajo.

Secret painting ceremony
A shaman first diagnoses what the patient is suffering from and then decides which of the many legends refer to that particular illness, and which of the many sand paintings he or she will use to represent it.

The ceremony takes place within a hogan, a traditional dwelling, where the shaman assembles the materials he or she needs and a number of painters. The painters carefully smooth the sand on the floor, then outline a design according to the shaman's instructions. Most designs are symmetrical, with an opening to the east—the direction of new life.

A Navajo sand painting ceremony in 1906, with a patient sitting on a sand painting next to a shaman.

The patient sits at the center of the painting, and the shaman begins to chant the story of the Sacred Beings. The shaman must not make a single mistake, since this would disturb the harmony he or she is trying to create. While chanting, the shaman moves across the sand painting, taking small handfuls of the colored powders and placing them on the body of the patient. In this way he or she transfers the power in the painting to the patient.

Most sand-painting ceremonies take place at night and must be completed before dawn, when the painting is completely destroyed. This is done so there is no trace of the painting left that could be used for the wrong purposes. When the ceremony lasts two or more days, a new painting is made each day.

Because of the sacred and secret nature of sand paintings, only a few people outside the Navajo have ever seen one. Those shown in museums or depicted in Navajo weaving have all been changed in some way so they are no longer thought powerful. Sometimes they are reversed, or important details of the legends are deliberately left out.

Curriculum Context

Many curricula ask students to compare attitudes toward the natural environment in different cultures. The Navajo believe their land is sacred and they have a responsibility to care for it.

Shamanism

Scholars use the term "shamanism" to describe a type of religious practice followed by many Native American peoples, but the word *shaman* is not Native American. It comes from the Tungus people of Siberia and means "wise one." European colonists and explorers who saw shamans curing the sick often described them as "medicine men" or "medicine women" instead.

However, shamans' skill as healers were only one of the abilities they possessed. They were also believed to be capable of discovering lost property and of bringing animals close to the camps so that hunting would be easier. Shamans were also thought to have the power to control the weather.

Because of their skills in curing and in controlling matters that were essential to the people's survival, the shamans were often very powerful members of their communities. The famous leader of the Hunkpapa Sioux, Sitting Bull, was actually a shaman rather than a chief.

This photograph of a Navajo shaman was taken in 1872. Navajo shamans had an important role in the Navajo community, performing elaborate healing rituals involving chanting and sand painting.

The supernatural world

The shamans were thought to be capable of doing so many different things because of the influence they had with the spirits of the supernatural world. In Native American belief everything has a spirit, or soul. This spirit can be persuaded to use its power for the people's benefit when asked to do so by a shaman acting on behalf of the community.

A shaman often made contact with spirits after undergoing long periods of fasting, thirsting, and loss of sleep. When these experiences were over, the shaman entered a comalike state, or trance, in which he or she experienced dreams, or visions, in which spirits gave advice or warnings.

Becoming a shaman

Only certain people were able to become shamans. They were usually highly perceptive individuals. However, gaining shamanic ability was a long and difficult process that demanded stamina and courage. This was because the spirit allies, or guides, of the shamans tested them in many ways. These tests could take the form of sickness for the shaman or his or her family, terrible nightmares, or other ordeals. Only by passing these tests could the shaman progress to higher levels of spiritual awareness.

Curriculum Context

Students learning about belief systems in different societies could explore the relationship between shamans and the supernatural world, as expressed in beliefs around the world.

Shamanism and Christianity

Shamans had powerful positions in their societies and were in harmony with the spiritual world of Native Americans. For these reasons European priests and missionaries often considered the shamans to be the main opposition to the conversion of native peoples to Christianity. To the priests and missionaries the legends the shamans retold and the visions they experienced were beliefs that had to be stamped out and replaced by Christian ideas. They sometimes claimed the shamans were wizards and witches who were helped by the Devil, although the idea of a "devil" was European and not something that Native Americans believed in.

Shaman's rattles from about 1900. Shamans used rattles to communicate with the spirits in their healing rituals and ceremonies.

Persecution of shamans

Shamans have been persecuted for their beliefs since the time of early European contact in the 15th century. This continued under U.S. domination in the 19th and early 20th centuries. It was not until the Indian Religion Freedom Act of 1934 that practicing shamanism without fear of persecution was recognized as a legal right of Native Americans living in the United States.

A spiritual alternative

Since the 1960s and 1970s shamanism has become popular with many nonnative people who see it as an escape from the material demands of modern society and as a way of leading a more spiritual life.

On a different level, Native American shamans have begun working very successfully with professional hospital staff, treating both Native American and nonnative patients.

In modern tribal communities shamans are once again regarded as important. By retelling ancient legends and acting out tribal rituals, shamans are ensuring that future generations of Native Americans will not forget the traditions of their ancestors.

Sun Dance

The Sun Dance was an annual ceremony for many of the Great Plains tribes. Its name comes from a Siouan ritual called "Gazing at the Sun," but it had little to do with sun worship. It took place in the fall, when nomadic bands or family groups of hunters gathered to celebrate and to perform rituals that they believed renewed the world.

Although the Sun Dance originated with the Sioux, many other tribes had similar renewal rituals and adopted aspects of the Sioux Sun Dance. The most important of these was that the participants danced to drumbeats and songs that they believed matched the natural rhythm of the universe and encouraged growth and fertility.

They used a buffalo skull as an altar to emphasize their link with the animal on which their survival depended. They also put up a pole—a specially cut tree—at the center of a lodge to express their connection with nature and to pay respect to all growing things.

Skewers and thongs

Nonnative observers in the 19th century noted that some Sun Dancers attached themselves to the pole with thongs tied to skewers inserted through the skin on their chests.

By fasting (going without food or drink) for four days and then painfully tearing themselves free from the skewers—leaving scars they would bear for the rest of their lives—these Sun Dancers hoped to obtain a vision, or dream, that would benefit themselves and their people. Most Sun Dancers who suffered this ordeal did so because of a personal crisis—often the death of a wife, husband, or child. They believed that the pain would ease their sorrow.

A Cheyenne Sun Dance taking place in 1910. The Sun Dance was an occasion for socializing with other bands, arranging marriages, feasting, dancing, and holding a great buffalo hunt.

Curriculum Context

Students may be asked to describe the effects of 19th-century federal Indian policy and the extent to which Native American societies have been able to preserve their traditional practices.

Government ban

White observers exaggerated the importance of self-torture in the Sun Dance, and the U.S. government regarded it as a barbaric ceremony that prevented native peoples from adopting Christianity. The government therefore banned Sun Dances in 1881. Many Plains peoples continued to hold them in secret, however, until in 1934 the ban was officially lifted.

Sun Dances today

Many Great Plains peoples still hold Sun Dances, both as rituals of spiritual renewal and as statements of tribal identity. Sun Dances today are usually held far from the public gaze, in remote reservation areas thought to be full of spiritual power. Leonard Peltier, a leading member of the radical American Indian Movement, took part in a Sun Dance on the Lakota Sioux reservation at Rosebud, South Dakota, in 1973. He said afterward, "I felt great for weeks… feeling that my body had been thoroughly cleansed inside and out."

Sweat Lodge

Sweat lodges are small steam-filled shelters that resemble saunas. They were originally used by shamans (medicine men and women) and ordinary members of Plains peoples in ceremonies intended to make contact with the spirit powers. The idea was that, by sweating profusely, participants purified their bodies. This then allowed them to experience visions.

Simple structures

Traditionally, sweat lodges were usually constructed out of animal skins or blankets draped over a wooden framework. Sometimes they were made by simply draping canvas over the branches of a cottonwood tree. The ease and speed with which they could be put up and taken down reflects the fact that they were used by nomads who needed to keep on the move.

To maintain a constant cloud of steam inside a sweat lodge, the shaman regularly poured water over rocks that had been heated in a fire pit. Those who sought a vision sat bare-chested and bare-legged inside the lodge and scraped the sweat off their skin with sticks.

Curriculum Context

In social science curricula, students are often asked to examine the ways in which a society's natural environment influences its rituals and practices.

A Nez Percé sweat lodge photographed in 1910. Sweat lodges have a framework of poles lashed together over a circular fire pit, then covered with skins or blankets.

Wallace Black Elk, a 20th-century leader of the Lakota Sioux, explained the importance of sweat lodges to his people as follows: "The sweat lodge is made of from 12 to 16 young willows, and these too have a lesson to teach us, for in the fall their leaves die and return to earth, but in the spring they come to life again. So too men die, but live again in the real world of Wakan-Tanka [Great Spirit], where there is nothing but the spirits of all things, and this true life we may know here on earth if we purify our bodies and minds."

The sweat lodge has an important spiritual significance in that it combines the four basic elements of traditional Plains cosmology: fire, air, water, and earth (in the form of the rocks). The darkness inside the lodge represents the lack of knowledge that people have of the ways of the spirit world.

Secret sweat lodges

Like many traditional Native American religious practices, sweat-lodge ceremonies were banned by the U.S. government following the final defeat of Native Americans in 1890 in the massacre at the Battle of Wounded Knee. Native Americans continued to use sweat lodges in secret, however. The ban was not lifted until 1934, after which sweat lodges quickly became popular once again.

Sweat lodges today

During the 1960s and 1970s sweat-lodge ceremonies were frequently held by Native Americans who were striving to reassert their tribal rights and traditional cultures. Today sweat lodges are popular with Native Americans everywhere and they have also become popular with some nonnative Americans.

Wounded Knee

The last major conflict between the U.S. government and Native Americans. It took place in 1890 on a reservation in South Dakota, where more than 200 Sioux men, women, and children were killed.

Taboos

In its widest sense a taboo is a ban on a particular action that is believed to be harmful to society or repugnant in some other way. For example, in most cultures around the world it is taboo to eat human flesh or to have sexual relations with a close relative such as a brother or sister. Such actions are usually forbidden by law, but many minor taboos are reinforced by communities, even though they are not officially laid down by law.

In traditional native cultures many actions were considered taboo because they might disrupt the correct relationship between the natural world and the spirit world. If broken, such a taboo could result in severe physical or emotional damage to the person who broke it, to members of his or her family, or even to his or her descendants a hundred years later. It could then be fixed only by performing certain ritual actions that restored the balance of powers between the spirit world and the human world.

Burial grounds, such as this one of a Tlingit shaman from the Northwest Coast, were taboo places for most Native Americans.

Such Native American taboos covered a range of actions. For example, among the Iglulik Inuit of Arctic Canada the list of taboos included: eating the breast of a caribou in summer; touching game within a certain period after recovering from an illness; combing one's hair shortly after giving birth; wearing clothes made of caribou hide while preparing ammunition for a hunt; and using the lamp of a dead person.

Death and taboos

Other taboos were associated with death and the world of the dead. Among the Navajo the husband of a woman who died could not become involved in an emotional relationship with another woman for one year after the death of his wife. He was not even allowed to court a woman for one year.

Other death taboos related to the belongings of the deceased. Among the Washo people of the Great Basin a dwelling in which a death occurred was abandoned or even burned down. Peoples of the Northwest Coast had to break a hole through the wall of a house in which a person had died in order to remove the body: on no account was the body to be taken out through the door. Native American burial grounds in general were taboo places, especially the platform graves of the Plains peoples.

Taboos about childbirth

Many traditional Native American taboos were connected to the female menstrual cycle and giving birth. This is a list of Cheyenne taboos put together by a white scholar in 1904: young men could not eat or drink from dishes or pots used by a menstruating woman; a menstruating woman could not touch any weapon, shield, or medicine bundle; a menstruating woman could not ride stallions, only mares; a menstruating woman could not enter a lodge containing a medicine bundle. Isolation in a special lodge was imposed on most tribal women each month during their period. Inuit women were also required to give birth alone in a separate hut or tent.

Hunting taboos

A great many Native American taboos related to hunting. Luck is a powerful factor in the pursuit of game—a sudden noise near the quarry, caused by another animal or by a rival hunting party, could easily make the difference between success and failure. To avoid such bad luck, it was essential not to break certain taboos.

Since Native Americans believed that the animals they hunted were powerful spirit beings, one of the most important taboos among hunting peoples was to treat their prey disrespectfully. Bragging about one's ability to catch animals risked incurring a period of bad luck for the group's hunters, since it implied that a mere human was wiser than a supernatural being.

After a successful hunt a prayer or chant might be recited over the body of the dead animal. This gave thanks to the spirit being that was present in the animal for allowing itself to be caught and asked it to return in a new form so that a future hunt could be successful, too. The Mistassini Cree of Canada placed the bones of a butchered bear on a raised platform similar to the kind used by many peoples of the Plains for their own dead. This was a mark of respect to ensure that scavengers did not scatter the remains.

Other Native American taboos

There were many other taboos among Native Americans relating to diverse activities, but all connected with the harmony between the natural and the spirit worlds. For example, the Apache believed that if a person leaned against a tree that had been struck by lightning, he or she would fall ill. Among the Pima people, if a person made fun of someone with a mental disability, he or she risked having the same fate befall his or her own child or one of his or her relatives.

Curriculum Context

The respect shown by Native American hunters toward their prey is an example of how beliefs about the natural environment influenced everyday practices.

Totem Pole

Most people know totem poles from their use in Hollywood movies as symbols of "Indianness." However, in reality the totem pole was used only among tribes of the Northwest Coast in British Columbia and southern Alaska. Indeed, the well-known free-standing carved pole is a late development. It dates only from the period after European trade contacts introduced metal woodworking tools.

Totem poles were originally elaborately carved and decorated supporting posts for houses. The poles bore symbols of an individual family's ancestry. In this sense they served a function similar to the coats of arms of knights in European history. Like the coats of arms, totem poles were a statement of family lineage.

Different uses

Over time Native Americans replaced their traditional woodcarving tools with more efficient iron tools obtained through trade with Europeans. The new tools enabled craftsmen to create larger totem poles.

Some poles served as ceremonial entrance posts to houses via an opening cut through their bases. Others were carved as free-standing posts to mark notable events. Totem poles might also have acted as memorials to individuals, with the carved crests depicting the various marriage ties between different families.

Family prestige

Totem poles were often associated with family prestige. Putting up a new pole was accompanied by feasts and distributions of gifts (known as potlatches) sponsored by the host family. The greater the honor being claimed, the larger the feasts and the more valuable the gifts. An extension of this was the putting up of ridicule posts, which one family would use to deride a rival family. Some totem poles were used as welcoming posts.

Curriculum Context

Students are often asked to describe the importance of family ties and family loyalty in different cultures and how these are expressed in a society's rituals and artistic output.

Carved poles depicting mythical figures—such as the Bear Mother—with outstretched palms assured visitors that their hosts carried no weapons and, therefore, presented no threat to their safety.

Totem poles today

During the 19th and early 20th centuries many totem poles were cut down at the insistence of religious authorities who felt that the poles undermined their efforts to convert native populations to Christianity. Other poles were taken to museums and totem-pole parks, where they stand today as a tribute to the age of Northwest Coast woodcarving.

However, the woodcarving art has survived. Recently there has been a resurgence in pole-carving combined with a greater sense of awareness and pride in Native American identity.

The carving of a bear shown here is part of a Tlingit totem pole in a state park in Ketchikan, Alaska.

Totemism

Common among native peoples, totemism is the belief that individuals can have a direct relationship with, or an ancestral link to, a particular spirit being, or totem. Sometimes several individuals in a clan (a group of families) share the same totem. The word totem comes from the Ojibway (Chippewa) word *ototeman*, meaning "relatives."

Medicine bundle

A collection of objects normally kept in a pouch made from animal or bird skin. Medicine bundles served as symbols linking the owner to animal spirits.

Orenda

Mystical or supernatural power believed by the Iroquois to be present in all objects and living things.

Native Americans frequently portray their totems in carvings and paintings as animals or birds. They also often include their symbols in medicine bundles, in the form of fur or feathers.

The exact form of totems varies widely from tribe to tribe and between cultural areas. At their simplest level, totems are thought of as personal guardians or helpers and are often associated with shamans (medicine men and women). Shamans' totems also vary widely—each shaman has his or her own totem that he or she considers to be a source of power.

Warriors also used personal totems, but these tended to be more similar to each other and were usually related to animals that had skills a warrior needed or desired. A warrior might be inspired by a turtle, for example, because turtles were supposed to be difficult to kill.

Elaborate totems are common in the Subarctic and Woodland regions. The Iroquois, for example, have bear clans and wolf clans to which many people belong. They believe they share a common bond with these animals and that clan members benefit from their virtues. They consider bears to be spiritually powerful and believe that bear-clan people can wield orenda most effectively. Wolves are renowned for their cooperative hunting skills and were once associated with warriors.

The best-known symbols of totemism are the carved totem poles put up by the tribes of the Northwest Coast. They represent both clan and family lineages (lines of descent) and depict, in animal form, spirits that are said to have helped the mythical founding ancestors of the clan and family. A family's totem pole may prominently show both the clan's totem—in the form of an eagle, for example—and the family totem, in the form of, say, a beaver.

Totemism today

Many Native Americans continue to place special importance on totems as a way of connecting with traditional values that have been handed down through the generations. In this way their totems serve as a reminder of tribal identity and pride, separate from the European traditions and beliefs that dominate modern North American culture.

The carved totem poles of the Northwest Coast are among the finest woodcarvings produced by Native Americans.

Vision Quest

A Vision Quest is an attempt by an individual to gain the help of a supernatural being to solve a particular problem or to provide general guidance over a lifetime. Vision Quests are more common among Native Americans who originally lived east of the Rockies than among those who lived west of the mountain range. They are particularly associated with the peoples of the Plains, such as the Shoshoni, Cheyenne, and Lakota Sioux.

Curriculum Context

Students learning about the folklore traditions of different societies might choose to focus on Vision Quests and what they reveal about spiritual beliefs among native peoples.

A test of mind and body

A Vision Quest is an intensely sacred activity. It is not undertaken lightly because it involves a great deal of physical and psychological stress. Although some people are thought capable of receiving a vision more easily than others, most people seeking a vision need the advice and help of a shaman (a medicine man or woman). Under the guidance of the shaman the vision-seeker does a great deal of ritual preparation.

The first stage is for the vision-seeker to gather various items that the shaman requires. They may include different scented grasses and herbs, particular stones or other minerals, and sometimes the feathers or skin of specific birds or animals. Tobacco is also necessary for the vision-seeker and the shaman to smoke as a prayer offering to the spirits with whom contact is sought. All these items have to be ritually prepared and blessed before they can be used.

The next step is for the vision-seeker to undergo a purification ritual. Native Americans believe that to attempt to approach the spirit world in an unpurified state is highly dangerous. Purification can involve taking a sweat bath, drinking an herbal concoction that causes vomiting, or undergoing smudging—burning a sacred material, such as cedar wood, sage, or sweetgrass, and blowing the smoke over the body.

A Cheyenne sweat lodge frame from 1910. Purification in a sweat lodge was an important part of the Vision Quest ritual. A buffalo skull was often placed in front of the lodge, forming a sacred path and facilitating the entrance of the spirits.

During and after purification the vision-seeker prays constantly. These prayers are requests for the strength to withstand the power of the supernatural world should it come in a vision.

Finally, the vision-seeker goes into the wilderness to fast (go without food or drink) and chant and possibly go without sleep. The vision-seeker looks for a place far away from other people, such as the top of a high mesa, or a dangerous place, such as a path frequently used by bears. In this way the vision-seeker demonstrates the sacrifices he or she is prepared to make and the dangers he or she is willing to overcome in order to show faith in the power of the spirits.

The vision, when it comes, gives a clear indication to the seeker about what to do next. Often the spirit appears in the form of a bird or animal, which instructs the seeker on how best to live and what precautions to take when next approaching the spirit world. Often, it also gives him or her a song and ways to paint the face and body when next trying to contact the spirit.

Curriculum Context

A Vision Quest reflects an individual's faith in the power of the spirits. The ritual reflects the central beliefs of the Plains peoples.

Women

With few exceptions, popular images of Native American women are of semifictional and romanticized heroines, such as Pocahontas, or of passive figures in a world dominated by male chiefs, warriors, and male shamans, or medicine men. The reality for most women in traditional Native American households was very different from these stereotypes and remains so today.

In present-day Native American communities, women frequently hold positions of real power and authority. This was true in the past, too, even among warlike peoples such as the Natchez and the Iroquois.

Matriarchy

A social system in which a mother is seen as the head of the family or tribe and descent is traced through the female line.

Positions of authority

Both the Natchez and Iroquois practiced matriarchy. Positions of responsibility were handed down through the female line—although the exercise of that authority was often a male activity. Among the Natchez, for example, children inherited their status from their mothers, even though the tribal leader and chief priest was a man who was obliged to marry beneath his rank.

The Iroquoian system gave a fundamental role to Clan Mothers, or Beloved Women, who were heads of multifamily households. Although women did not sit on Iroquois councils where tribal decisions were made, the Beloved Women appointed the male representatives of the different households. They also had the power to remove a man from such a position through a ceremony called dehorning—removing his horned headdress, which served as a badge of office—if they felt he was failing in his duty.

Curriculum Context

Students asked to compare the status and role of women in different societies could focus on the role of Clan Mothers in the Iroquois matriarchal system.

Even in other Native American communities women played an active role. When the first Europeans made contact with Plains peoples, they formed the impression that the women's role was an inferior one. They noticed that the women walked demurely a few paces behind the men and took no apparent part in making decisions. But this was only because the European observers were invariably themselves men, and Plains etiquette demanded they be received, feasted, and invited to sit in council meetings with only the leading men of the tribe.

In fact many Plains tribesmen owned little more than their clothing, weapons, and a war pony. Everything else—the home, its furnishings, the everyday riding horses, even the meat brought back to camp from a hunt—was the woman's property, for her to use or dispose of as she saw fit.

The important, even exalted, position of women in Native American society can be seen in their roles in folklore. Among farming tribes the Corn Mother, or Corn Woman, is the essential female symbol and is often credited with giving the tribe life. Even among hunting peoples it is a female spirit—in the form of Buffalo Woman or, among the Inuit, as Sedna, the goddess of fish and game animals—who can cause famine if she is displeased because the people are disrespectful or failing in their ritual duties.

Folklore
The traditional beliefs, customs, tales, and myths of a people, handed down from one generation to the next.

Elsewhere the male Trickster or Transformer—often called Coyote or Old Man Coyote—was seen as being responsible for giving people life and providing the animals and plants on which they depended. Yet he is often fooled by female spirits.

In Blackfoot tales, for example, Napi, or Old Man, breathes life into clay figures of a man and woman that he has made. But Old Woman insists she must always have the last say regarding all Napi's decisions. So she is able to modify what he wants and decides what form the people should take and how they should live. Similarly, at the end of Blackfoot Trickster stories Napi attempts to fool the Woman Chief, but she defeats him and turns him into a pine tree.

Powerful medicine women

In addition to the mythic and religious significance of women, it was widely believed by Native Americans that some women had healing powers that were often more powerful than those of medicine men. This power brought them respect as shamans, or medicine women. Such women were considered to be able to undergo spiritual tests and hardships too daunting for many male shamans.

Men also thought that this power brought women into contact with dangerous forces that could weaken some of the most powerful medicines used by medicine men. There was a widespread fear among men that to anger a woman—particularly an elder—might bring

A female shaman from the Hupa of northwestern California, photographed in 1923. In some Californian groups, female shamans were thought to be more powerful and skilled practitioners of the healing arts than male shamans.

swift retribution on the offender in the form of an accident, illness, or other personal disaster. For this reason, when Native American men addressed a woman as Grandmother, they did so with great respect for her as a life-giver and carer but also with a degree of unease and caution.

The role of women today

In present-day native communities women are expected to fulfill several roles. They are often seen by men not only as homemakers whose role it is to tackle family problems, but also as being responsible for dealing with issues of wider social, and at times political, significance. Many native women's groups are especially active in dealing with often complex and longstanding problems of the tribal homelands, whether on reservations or in urban communities.

That women have an influential voice in modern Native American society is reflected in the fact that increasing numbers of them are expressing themselves as novelists and poets. There is now a large and growing body of contemporary Native American women's literature.

Many Native American women today are involved in education, too, frequently at university level. They are also actively involved in various areas of community service and with different self-help groups.

Native American women continue to play an active and vital part in the ritual and spiritual lives of their communities. And they are often a driving force in restoring a sense of Native American pride, unity, and achievement against frequently difficult odds.

Curriculum Context

In studies of the role of women in past and present cultures, students may be asked to consider changes in women's roles and ways in which roles have remained the same.

Glossary

Amulet An object worn as a charm to protect the wearer against evil.

Aztec Term used to describe the people who were dominant in central Mexico before the Spanish conquest in the 16th century.

Bloodletting The practice of removing blood from a person's body, usually in order to prevent or cure illness.

Chickee A Seminole house built on stilts, with a log frame, open sides, and a thatched roof over a raised wooden platform. *Chickee* is the Seminole word for house.

Clan A social unit consisting of a number of households or families with a common ancestor.

Folklore The traditional beliefs, customs, tales, and myths of a people, handed down from one generation to the next.

Gorget A piece of armor used to protect the throat.

Grave goods Objects left with the body of a deceased person at the time of burial or cremation. The practice of placing goods with the dead was common in many cultures and beliefs about their purpose varied. Examples included personal possessions of the deceased, textiles, weapons, pottery, and jewelry.

Hogan A traditional Navajo dwelling and site of religious ceremonies. The Navajo believe that hogans are one of the most sacred places, binding the people to their land.

Hoop and pole A game in which a hoop with marked segments is rolled along the ground while a player attempts to hit it with a spear or arrow. Points are scored according to which segment the spear or arrow hits.

Hunter–gatherers People who obtain most of their food by hunting wild animals and eating plants gathered from the wild.

Kachina A deified spirit believed by the Hopi and other Pueblo peoples to be the ancestor of a human. The term also describes the masked dancers who impersonated the spirits in ceremonies and small wooden dolls that were representations of the spirits.

Kiva In Pueblo villages, a chamber built into the ground that acts as a meeting place and ceremonial house.

Mandala A circular design representing the universe.

Matriarchy A social system in which a mother is seen as the head of the family or tribe and descent is traced through the female line.

Medicine bundle A collection of objects normally kept in a pouch made from animal or bird skin. Medicine bundles served as symbols linking the owner to animal spirits.

Mesoamerica The cultural area extending from central Mexico to Nicaragua.

Minipoka In some Native-American groups, a favored child, usually the son or daughter of a wealthy and respected family.

Moiety One of two units into which a tribe or community is divided on the basis of descent through one line to a common ancestor.

Orenda Mystical or supernatural power believed by the Iroquois to be present in all objects and living things.

Powwow A gathering of Native Americans, often involving feasting and dancing. The word comes from the Narragansett word *powwaw*, meaning shaman or magician.

Prayer stick A stick used by Pueblo peoples for prayers and in ceremonies. Feathers were attached to prayer sticks as offerings to the spirits.

Pueblo peoples Village-dwelling peoples of the Southwest, including present-day New Mexico and Arizona.

Roach A hairstyle in which the head is shaved except for a strip from front to back across the top of the head.

Sacred Beings In Navajo religion, spiritual beings who created humans.

Scaffold In some Native American cultures, a raised platform on which the body of a dead person was left to decompose.

Scalping Removing the skin from the head of a dead enemy, usually with its attached hair, as a battle trophy.

Shaman A person with special powers to access the spirit world and an ability to use magic to heal the sick and control events.

Sipapu A small circular hole in the floor of a kiva that is a symbol of the hole through which the very first people emerged into the present world.

Sun Dance An important ceremony practiced by Plains peoples to celebrate the renewal of nature.

Sweat lodge A steam-filled shelter used in ceremonies undertaken to make contact with the spirits.

Tepee A cone-shaped tent built with a pole framework and traditionally covered with animal skins.

Trickster In the folklore, mythology, and religion of some societies, a mischievous and cunning god or spirit.

Vision Quest A rite of passage in many Native American groups, in which young individuals went alone to an isolated place to seek protection from the spirits.

Wampum belt A decorative belt made from small cylindrical beads made from polished shells. The belts were used for ceremonial purposes and to record important events.

Wigwam A domed dwelling consisting of a single room, formed by a frame of arched poles and covered with a roofing material such as birchbark, grass, or hides.

Wounded Knee The last major conflict between the U.S. government and Native Americans. It took place in 1890 on a reservation in South Dakota, where more than 200 Sioux men, women, and children were killed.

Further Research

BOOKS

Basel, Roberta. *Sequoyah: Inventor of Written Cherokee*. "Signature Lives" series. Compass Point Books, 2008.

Blaisdell, Bob (ed.). *Great Speeches by Native Americans*. Dover Publications, 2000.

Brown, Joseph Epes, and Emily Cousins. *Teaching Spirits: Understanding Native American Religious Traditions*. Oxford University Press, 2001.

Doherty, Craig A., and Katherine M. Doherty. *Northeast Indians*. Chelsea House Publications, 2008.

Eastman, Charles A., and Ohiyesa. *Indian Boyhood*. Book Jungle, 2007.

Fitzgerald, Judith, and Michael Oren Fitzgerald (eds.). *Indian Spirit*. World Wisdom, revised edition, 2006.

Fitzgerald, Michael Oren. *Yellowtail, Crow Medicine Man and Sun Dance Chief: An Autobiography*. University of Oklahoma Press, 1994.

Glatzer, Jenna. *Native American Festivals and Ceremonies*, "Native American Life" series. Mason Crest Publishers, illustrated edition, 2002.

Native American Literature. Glencoe/McGraw-Hill, 2001.

Hartz, Paula. *Native American Religions*, "World Religions" series. Facts on File, updated edition, 2004.

Hinshaw Patent, Dorothy. *The Buffalo and the Indians: A Shared Destiny*. Clarion Books, 2006.

Johnson, Michael. *Encyclopedia of Native Tribes of North America*. Firefly Books, 2007.

Lurie, Nancy. *Mountain Wolf Woman, Sister of Crashing Thunder: The Autobiography of a Winnebago Indian*. University of Michigan Press/Regional, 1961.

Lynch, Patricia Ann. *Native American Mythology A to Z*. Facts on File, 2004.

Montgomery, David R. *Crafts and Skills of the Native Americans*. Skyhorse Publishing, 2009.

Neihardt, John G. *Black Elk Speaks: Being the Life Story of a Holy Man of the Oglala Sioux*. State University of New York Press, annotated edition, 2008.

Penney, David W., and George Horse Capture. *North American Indian Art*, "World of Art" series. Thames & Hudson, 2004.

Philip, Neil. *A Braid of Lives: Native American Childhood*. Clarion Books, 2000.

Philip, Neil. *The Great Mystery: Myths of Native America*. Clarion Books, 2001.

Pritzker, Barry M. *A Native American Encyclopedia: History, Culture, and Peoples*. Oxford University Press, 2000.

Roop, Peter, and Connie Roop. *Sitting Bull*. Scholastic, 2002.

Waldman, Carl, and Molly Braun. *Encyclopedia of Native American Tribes*. Facts on File, third edition, 2006.

Wilcox, Charlotte. *The Iroquois*, "Native American Histories" series. Lerner Publications, 2006.
.

INTERNET RESOURCES

NativeAmericans.com. A comprehensive site with information and links about all aspects of Native American culture, beliefs, art, and history.
www.nativeamericans.com

Smithsonian: American Indian History and Culture. A Smithsonian Institution website, with information about all aspects of Native American culture.
www.si.edu/Encyclopedia_SI/History_and_Culture/AmericanIndian_History.htm

National Museum of the American Indian. The website of the Smithsonian Institution's National Museum of the American Indian. The site provides information about the museum's collections as well as educational resources for students about the history and culture of Native Americans.
www.nmai.si.edu/

NativeWeb. A website with links to all aspects of Native American studies.
www.nativeweb.org/

NativeTech. A resource focusing on the arts of the Eastern Woodland peoples, with links to information about beadwork, featherwork, games, clothes, and pottery.
www.nativetech.org

American Indians and the Natural World. A website of the Carnegie Museum of Natural History, with information on different beliefs about the natural world among the Tlingit of the Norwest Coast, the Hopi of the Southwest, the Iroquois of the Northeast, and the Lakota of the Plains.
www.carnegiemnh.org//exhibits/north-south-east-west/

Index

Page numbers in *italic* refer to illustrations.

39.95   4/21/10